A GAZE OF LOVE

A Gaze of Love

Encountering God Within

SHIRLEY SULLIVAN

ST PAULS

Library of Congress Cataloging-in-Publication Data

Sullivan, Shirley Darcus, 1945-
   A gaze of love : encountering God within / Shirley Sullivan.
        p. cm.
   Includes bibliographical references and index.
   ISBN-13: 978-0-8189-1279-5
   ISBN-10: 0-8189-1279-0
   1. Spirituality—Catholic Church. 2. Spiritual life—Catholic Church.   I. Title.
   BX2350.65.S88   2008
   248.4'82—dc22

                                        2008031108

Produced and designed in the United States of America by the
Fathers and Brothers of the Society of St. Paul,
2187 Victory Boulevard, Staten Island, NY 10314-6603
as part of their communications apostolate.

ISBN-10: 0-8189-1279-0
ISBN-13: 978-0-8189-1279-5

Printing Information:

Current Printing - first digit   1   2   3   4   5   6   7   8   9   10

Year of Current Printing - first year shown
2009   2010   2011   2012   2013   2014   2015   2016   2017   2018

Dedication

For Mary
Mater Thesauri Cordis

TABLE OF CONTENTS

PREFACE

This book discusses how people can come to discover and to relate to the presence of God within their own souls. All too often it has been mistakenly assumed that knowledge and experience of this indwelling of God is reserved for people who live a consecrated life in different contemplative orders. Certainly such people may live with a vivid awareness of the divine presence but what they know and live is available also for Christians living in the world. God extends his invitation to many! Spiritual writers often remind us that the encounter in deep prayer with God is a gift, a grace that can be granted but never demanded. How true this is! But it is also true that God calls many to dwell in inner stillness in the depths of their being. The aim of this book is to suggest ways in which we can come to respond eagerly to this invitation and to encounter the divine indwelling in a gaze of love.

First, an important point. Who is this God who abides in human beings? In this book, in references to God, I will use, for ease of reading, pronouns such as "he," "him," "his" etc. but will urge all readers to keep ever in mind that, as Jesus told us, "God is spirit" (Jn 4:24). God's nature is infinite and ineffable. What is truly amazing is that this God, so far beyond our comprehension or expression, deigns to dwell within us.

Second, how will we approach this topic? Crucial to the discovery of the divine presence within and a response to that presence is an understanding of our human nature. We will suggest that in particular the human will holds the key to finding God within. We will, therefore, discuss in full the nature of this will, illustrating aspects of it through examination of various passages from Scripture.

We hope that the chapters that follow will encourage many to surrender in trust and confidence to God within. God longs for us to become "a glorious crown in the hand of the Lord, a royal diadem held by your God" (Is 62:3). One way in which these longings can be fulfilled is by our finding God within and surrendering to his presence there.

Biblical Abbreviations

OLD TESTAMENT

Genesis	Gn	Nehemiah	Ne	Baruch	Ba
Exodus	Ex	Tobit	Tb	Ezekiel	Ezk
Leviticus	Lv	Judith	Jdt	Daniel	Dn
Numbers	Nb	Esther	Est	Hosea	Ho
Deuteronomy	Dt	1 Maccabees	1 M	Joel	Jl
Joshua	Jos	2 Maccabees	2 M	Amos	Am
Judges	Jg	Job	Jb	Obadiah	Ob
Ruth	Rt	Psalms	Ps	Jonah	Jon
1 Samuel	1 S	Proverbs	Pr	Micah	Mi
2 Samuel	2 S	Ecclesiastes	Ec	Nahum	Na
1 Kings	1 K	Song of Songs	Sg	Habakkuk	Hab
2 Kings	2 K	Wisdom	Ws	Zephaniah	Zp
1 Chronicles	1 Ch	Sirach	Si	Haggai	Hg
2 Chronicles	2 Ch	Isaiah	Is	Malachi	Ml
Ezra	Ezr	Jeremiah	Jr	Zechariah	Zc
		Lamentations	Lm		

NEW TESTAMENT

Matthew	Mt	Ephesians	Eph	Hebrews	Heb
Mark	Mk	Philippians	Ph	James	Jm
Luke	Lk	Colossians	Col	1 Peter	1 P
John	Jn	1 Thessalonians	1 Th	2 Peter	2 P
Acts	Ac	2 Thessalonians	2 Th	1 John	1 Jn
Romans	Rm	1 Timothy	1 Tm	2 John	2 Jn
1 Corinthians	1 Cor	2 Timothy	2 Tm	3 John	3 Jn
2 Corinthians	2 Cor	Titus	Tt	Jude	Jude
Galatians	Gal	Philemon	Phm	Revelation	Rv

A GAZE OF LOVE

THE CHRISTIAN CALLING

*T*here is a well-known story about the Curé d'Ars who, on being asked how he could spend hours in Church before the tabernacle, said quietly: "He looks at me and I look at Him."[1] In the amazing simplicity of this answer we behold the truth of a soul completely surrendered in love for and adoration of Jesus. All Christians are called to such a love-relationship with God. And the truth is even more astounding than this one revealed in the life of the Curé d'Ars. We need not go to a church to encounter and to love God. We need only go deep within our own souls and gaze on him in love there. What a mystery is here! What a truth to make us dance! Yet, can this be true? Scripture assures us that it is so.

The Divine Indwelling

Before he ascended to be with the Father, Jesus made promises to his followers of his continued presence with them. At the end of Matthew's Gospel he says (28:20): "And behold, I am

---

[1] On the Curé d'Ars see L. Sheppard, *Portrait of a Parish Priest* (London: Burns & Oates, 1958) and Abbé F. Trochu, *Curé d'Ars* (Rockport, IL: TAN Books, 1977).

with you always, until the end of the age." In John's Gospel Jesus speaks more fully of his abiding presence with us (14:15-23):

> "If you love me, you will keep my commandments. And I will ask the Father, and he will give you another Advocate to be with you always, the Spirit of truth, which the world cannot accept, because it neither sees nor knows it. But you know it, because it remains with you, and will be in you. I will not leave you orphans; I will come to you. In a little while the world will no longer see me, but you will see me, because I live and you will live. On that day you will realize that I am in my Father and you are in me and I am in you. Whoever has my commandments and observes them is the one who loves me. And whoever loves me will be loved by my Father, and I will love him and reveal myself to him." Judas, not the Iscariot, said to him, "Master, then what happened that you will reveal yourself to us and not to the world?" Jesus answered and said to him, "Whoever loves me will keep my word, and my Father will love him, and we will come to him and make our dwelling with him."

In Matthew then we hear that Jesus will always be with us. In John Jesus promises to send the "Spirit of truth," which will "remain" in us and "be" in us. He also says that he "will come" to us. He tells us that, once he has ascended, we will realize that he is "in the Father" and we "are" in him and he "is" in us. To those who love him, Jesus says he will "reveal" himself. He then promises that to those who "keep" his word, both he and the Father "will come" and "make their dwelling" with them.

A close examination of this passage of John teaches us a vital truth: Jesus promises that the Trinity will dwell within us.

He mentions the Holy Spirit, the "Spirit of truth," his Father, and himself as being with us. Jesus makes clear that the requirement for this indwelling of God is that people "love" him, saying that those who do love him also keep his commandments. Jesus had given his disciples one main "new" commandment (Jn 13:34-35)[2]:

> I give you a new commandment: love one another. As
> I have loved you, so you also should love one another.
> This is how all will know that you are my disciples, if
> you have love for one another.

Those who love Jesus will also love one another. In people loving in this way, the Trinity will come and abide.

It is wonderful to hear that this privilege of the divine indwelling will be given to us Christians. But, on hearing this, we may find ourselves asking some questions: Do I find God within? How am I to find God within? Is God truly there? We may also realize that the answers to these questions are not readily available. We may admit that, however much we may want to find God in our souls, we do not in fact encounter him there. Or, it may be, that we find God within on some occasions but we do not consistently find him there. We may strongly wish to follow Jesus' exhortation to "remain" in him (Jn 15:4-9) but simply do not know how to do so.

Background

Essential to our discovery of the divine indwelling is an understanding of the nature of human beings and the call we receive as Christians. In this regard an essential feature of us as

---

[2]   Cf. also the call to "love one another" in Jn 15:12-17.

human beings is that we possess free will. This gift of free will is perhaps the most valuable treasure God bestowed on human nature. In Genesis we hear of the formation of human beings (1:26-27):

> Then God said: "Let us make human beings in our image, after our likeness. Let them have dominion over the fish of the sea, the birds of the air, and the cattle, and over all the wild animals and all the creatures that crawl on the ground." God created human beings in his image; in the divine image he created them; male and female he created them.

People have pondered for centuries what the exact nature of this "divine image" might be and it may be that we will never fully understand the mystery of this passage. But one suggestion we can make is that part at least of this "divine image" consists of our possession of free will. God is entirely free. Each Person of the Trinity loves freely.

During each moment of our life, we too have the freedom to choose our actions. We never have to teach our children to express this freedom. From their earliest days they show that they are born with it. Scripture tells us in the story of Adam and Eve that the human capacity for free will led to the radical change in our circumstances. Endowed with the freedom to choose to obey God or not, Eve and then Adam chose not to do so. Let us look at the passage in Genesis that describes their activities (3:1-6):

> Now the serpent was the most cunning of all the animals that the Lord God had made. The serpent asked the woman, "Did God really tell you not to eat from any of the trees in the garden?" The woman answered the serpent: "We may eat of the fruit of the trees in

the garden; it is only about the fruit of the tree in the middle of the garden that God said, 'You shall not eat it or even touch it, lest you die.'" But the serpent said to the woman: "You certainly will not die! No, God knows well that the moment you eat of it your eyes will be opened and you will be like gods who know what is good and what is bad." The woman saw that the tree was good for food, pleasing to the eyes, and desirable for gaining wisdom. So she took some of its fruit and ate it; and she also gave some to her husband, who was with her, and he ate it.

What choices do we see Eve making here? First, she listens to the serpent rather than trusting in what God had told her. The serpent promises knowledge of "good" and "bad" in contrast to God who had warned her about death. We human beings want good things for ourselves and sometimes the desire for them outweighs our fear of evil. Second, Eve ponders the choice she has to make. The fruit looks delicious; it was attractive. Most of all, it would, it seems, give "wisdom."

This last point is the crucial one in Eve's decision. The serpent had spoken of her "knowing what is good and what is bad." Adam and Eve thus far do not know what both these two things are. Up until this moment, their experience has been only of the good. Why would they want to know "what is bad"? Why does Eve acquaint such knowledge with "wisdom"? Here is the core of the nature of human free will. There is something in us that desires to know the whole range of experience. Warnings do not work to prevent us from choosing what may harm us greatly. We consciously reach for forbidden fruit, as Eve did. We are impatient and, whatever we desire, we want right away. Just like Eve, we listen to our own assessment of the value of things. As Eve did so, obedience was forgotten and her trust in God lost.

What we see happening with Eve we see happening often in our own lives. We each lose the Garden of Paradise by our own choices. How often, for example, do parents see their children choosing with determination what is harmful to them? All parents instinctively want to guard their children from pain and sorrow but all parents soon learn that there is a self-will in these children that will inevitably lead them to learn what suffering is. In a similar way, how frequently do we discern in ourselves an inclination to choose with abandon what we know is not the best course of action?

The misuse of human free will was certainly not part of God's plan for human beings but its possibility was inherent in the gift. Why then did God give us this gift? The answer is related to another way in which we appear to be made in the "divine image," one clearly related to the first. Human beings have freedom of choice and the most important choice they make is to love. By "love" I do not refer to the emotional feelings of affection of one human being for another. I refer instead to the human capacity to form, by choice, a positive relationship with another. In such a relationship there may well be strong feelings of affection but the core of the relationship is an act of will, not a response to feelings. The great *shema* of Judaism calls all human beings to follow one great commandment (Dt 6:5):

> Hear, O Israel! The Lord is our God, the Lord alone!
> Therefore, you shall love the Lord, your God,
>   with all your heart,
> and with all your soul, and with all your strength.

Jesus repeats this summons (Mk 12:28-31):

> One of the scribes, when he came forward and heard
> them disputing and saw how well he had answered

them, asked him, "Which is the first of all the commandments?" Jesus replied, "The first is this: 'Hear, O
Israel! The Lord our God is Lord alone! You shall love
the Lord your God with all your heart, with all your
soul, with all your mind, and with all your strength.'
The second is this: 'You shall love your neighbor as
yourself.' There is no other commandment greater
than these."

Obedience to these commands involves a choice of the will to
commit "heart, soul, and strength" to God and to treat other
people as we treat ourselves. It may be that this choice will include
feelings of affection for God and neighbor. But, especially in the
case of the latter, even if we find ourselves quite disliking someone, we can choose to treat that person with respect and honor.

All human beings recognize that only love that is freely
given, that is given by choice, is of any value. If we state this in
another way, we can say that only love that is freely given can
be called "love." In loving we choose to be kind, helpful, and
good to the beloved. We can never force anyone to love us. We
may often observe in a love relationship that the first stages are
strongly marked by a mutual attraction to the beauty in the other.
But as years go by and the flaws as well as the beauty in another
become apparent, loving becomes more difficult. Gradually then
love manifests itself in a more profound way as a commitment of
the will to the other. When two people make such a commitment
and they adhere to it day by day, they grow in a different kind
of beauty, namely in spiritual strength and devotion. Love then
itself becomes strong and sure, based on a firm decision of the
will to be faithful.

Let us look at the will in the Christian context. John sums
up our Christian faith in the following words of Jesus (3:13-16):

"No one has gone up to heaven except the one who has come down from heaven, the Son of Man. And just as Moses lifted up the serpent in the desert, so must the Son of Man be lifted up, so that everyone who believes in him may have eternal life." For God so loved the world that he gave his only Son, so that everyone who believes in him might not perish but might have eternal life.

Jesus tells us that he has come down from heaven in order that, through his passion and death on the cross, human beings may come, by faith in him, to have "eternal life." John then tells us that "God so loved the world" that he sent Jesus with this mission of salvation to all. The Christian message is living and true, as valid today as on that day on which Jesus spoke. What we can say is that God loves the world. God is in love with the world and by "world" we mean all human beings.

God has committed his will to save us, to restore what is beautiful in us and to make us his "children" (1 Jn 3:1). He accomplished this by allowing his Son to become the Paschal Lamb, sacrificed to take away our sins. He nurtures our spiritual life day by day by giving us Jesus as heavenly manna. The bread and wine at the Eucharist become the body and blood of Jesus, who then feeds us with himself. Not only this but God, by sending "the Spirit of his Son into our hearts" (Rm 5:5; Gal 4:6), allows us to share in the resurrected life of Jesus. What God has given us, therefore, is a very participation in the life of Jesus. Thus Jesus tells us clearly that we will have this new life (Jn 14:15-18):

If you love me, you will keep my commandments. And I will ask the Father, and he will give you another Advocate to be with you always, the Spirit of truth, which the world cannot accept, because it neither sees

nor knows it. But you know it, because it remains with
you, and will be in you. I will not leave you orphans;
I will come to you.

What effect do these truths have on our behavior and, in
particular, on the choices of our will? We no longer live under
the "old covenant" according to which human beings strove with
their wills to achieve holiness. It had become patently apparent
by the time of the coming of Jesus that human beings could not,
by their own efforts, be truly good. Jesus established a "new covenant" according to which human beings are transformed by a
free gift of grace, won by his suffering and death.

As Christians, we are no longer to attempt to be justified by
the law, as St. Paul makes clear in Romans 3:19-26:

> Now we know that what the law says is addressed
> to those under the law, so that every mouth may be
> silenced and the whole world stand accountable to
> God, since no human being will be justified in his sight
> by observing the law; for through the law comes con-
> sciousness of sin. But now the righteousness of God has
> been manifested apart from the law, though testified to
> by the law and the prophets, the righteousness of God
> through faith in Jesus Christ for all who believe. For
> there is no distinction; all have sinned and are deprived
> of the glory of God. They are justified freely by his
> grace through the redemption in Christ Jesus, whom
> God set forth as an expiation, through faith, by his
> blood, to prove his righteousness because of the for-
> giveness of sins previously committed, through the for-
> bearance of God — to prove his righteousness in the
> present time, that he might be righteous and justify the
> one who has faith in Jesus.

If we believe in Jesus, we receive the free gift of grace, won by his having become for us an "expiation" of all our sins. We can freely surrender to grace and allow it to transform us. God will "justify the one who has faith in Jesus," doing so "freely by his grace." What a gift is here! As St. Paul also says in Ephesians 1:7-8:

> In him we have redemption by his blood, the forgiveness of transgressions, in accord with the riches of his grace that [God] lavished upon us.

God "lavishes" his grace upon us so that we can be transformed as human beings. Thus St. Paul says (Eph 2:8-10):

> For by grace you have been saved through faith, and this is not from you; it is the gift of God; it is not from works, so no one may boast. For we are his handiwork, created in Christ Jesus for the good works that God has prepared in advance, that we should live in them.

We are now a new "handiwork" of God, "created in Christ Jesus" and prepared to perform many "good works." God never ceases to pour this grace on his people, as St. Paul also makes clear (2 Cor 4:15):

> ...grace bestowed in abundance on more and more people may cause thanksgiving to overflow for the glory of God.

To what, then, are we Christians called? How are we to use our gift of free will day by day? St. Peter tells us what we are to strive to do (2 P 3:18): "...grow in grace and in the knowledge of our Lord and Savior Jesus Christ."

The first requirement for growth in grace is to understand fully the nature of that grace. It is totally sufficient. We must learn, by inner discernment, to resist placing any trust in our own strength, in our own inclinations of will, and to surrender instead to the working of grace in our souls. St. Paul describes this process in 2 Corinthians 12:7-10:

> [Jesus] said to me, "My grace is sufficient for you, for power is made perfect in weakness." I will rather boast most gladly of my weaknesses, in order that the power of Christ may dwell with me. Therefore, I am content with weaknesses, insults, hardships, persecutions, and constraints, for the sake of Christ; for when I am weak, then I am strong.

Our spiritual development will involve a gradual perception of what is the nature of our inner self or ego, in what ways it masters our will with its desires and inclinations, and in what manner we need to learn to free our will from the control of self and to surrender it to grace. This process is usually a long one, which may involve much suffering as we learn to "deny" the self, as Jesus called us to do (Mt 16:24). St. Paul presents the process in very vivid terms in Galatians (2:19-21):

> For through the law I died to the law, so that I might live for God. I have been crucified with Christ; yet I live, no longer I, but Christ lives in me; insofar as I now live in the flesh, I live by faith in the Son of God who has loved me and given himself up for me. I do not nullify the grace of God; for if justification comes through the law, then Christ died for nothing.

By grace Jesus will live within us but, for that to occur, the self or ego in us must be resisted. St. Paul says that, even though he is alive, the life within him is that of Jesus, present by the grace of

God. He does not strive by effort of his will to achieve "justification" because, if that were possible, Jesus has "died for nothing." Instead, he allows grace to work in him, living "by faith in the Son of God." So we are all called to live.

How do we bring our wills to surrender to grace within our souls? Here our teacher is Jesus as St. Paul says (Ph 1:5-11):

> Have among yourselves the same attitude that is also yours in Christ Jesus, Who, though he was in the form of God, did not regard equality with God something to be grasped. Rather, he emptied himself, taking the form of a slave, coming in human likeness; and found human in appearance, he humbled himself, becoming obedient to death, even death on a cross. Because of this, God greatly exalted him and bestowed on him the name that is above every name, so that at the name of Jesus every knee should bend, of those in heaven and on earth and under the earth, and every tongue confess that Jesus Christ is Lord, to the glory of God the Father.

Our "attitude" is to be like that of Jesus. He "emptied" himself of all divinity when he came to earth and he then "emptied" himself even further, taking the lowest position among human beings. Jesus teaches us this "attitude" not only by his whole life but also by emptying himself each day as he becomes the bread and wine of the Eucharist. When we view the humble host, given to nurture and strengthen the life of grace within us, how can we not grasp clearly the path that we too should follow? Our call, therefore, is to "empty" ourselves of all self and ego, of all that sets us apart from or above others. We are so to guide and control our wills that they are ever surrendered to the working of grace in our souls.

But what does it mean to surrender the will to grace? Here we return to our discussion of love in which we suggested that love is an act of the will. It is gift freely given. As Christians, we are called to love Jesus, that is, to believe staunchly in him and all that he taught and to turn our wills steadfastly toward him, no matter what befalls us. St. Paul describes clearly what loving Jesus and surrendering our wills to grace may involve (2 Cor 4:6-11):

> For God who said, "Let light shine out of darkness," has shone in our hearts to bring to light the knowledge of the glory of God on the face of Jesus Christ. But we hold this treasure in earthen vessels, so that the surpassing power may be of God and not from us. We are afflicted in every way, but not constrained; perplexed, but not driven to despair; persecuted, but not abandoned; struck down, but not destroyed; always carrying about in the body the dying of Jesus, so that the life of Jesus may also be manifested in our body. For we who live are constantly being given up to death for the sake of Jesus, so that the life of Jesus may be manifested in our mortal flesh.

God has enlightened our hearts so that we recognize that Jesus is God. As we die to self, we bear the "dying of Jesus" in our bodies. As we allow Jesus to live in us, he is "manifested" in our bodies. We are just "earthen vessels," but God pours into us his "surpassing power," the presence of grace. In love we surrender our wills to Jesus within and, in so doing, we allow him to live in our souls and to radiate his light to others.

The principal thing, therefore, that we need to do is to love Jesus. We hear him asking us to love him. He wants us to live in him (Jn 15:1-5):

> I am the true vine, and my Father is the vine grower.
> He takes away every branch in me that does not bear
> fruit, and everyone that does he prunes so that it bears
> more fruit. You are already pruned because of the
> word that I spoke to you. Remain in me, as I remain
> in you. Just as a branch cannot bear fruit on its own
> unless it remains on the vine, so neither can you unless
> you remain in me. I am the vine, you are the branches.
> Whoever remains in me and I in him will bear much
> fruit, because without me you can do nothing.

We are to "remain" in Jesus. When we do, we can expect that the Father will prune us so that we can bear "much fruit." Only if we are in Jesus will we be able to do anything. We are to allow Jesus to work in us, just as the vine feeds its branches. More and more, therefore, we will need to love Jesus, that is, to direct our wills to him and act only from the inner guidance that he will give to us. Jesus tells us what will happen if we do love him (Jn 14:23):

> Whoever loves me will keep my word, and my Father
> will love him, and we will come to him and make our
> dwelling with him.

If we love Jesus, we will "keep" his word and both he and the Father will come to dwell within us. The more we surrender our wills to Jesus, therefore, as he dwells in his Spirit in our hearts, the more will the life of God fill our being. We will become "emptied" of self and filled with God. We will become what St. Paul describes as the "praise of the glory" of God's grace (Eph 1:3-14):

> Blessed be the God and Father of our Lord Jesus
> Christ, who has blessed us in Christ with every spiri-

tual blessing in the heavens, as he chose us in him, before the foundation of the world, to be holy and without blemish before him. In love he destined us for adoption to himself through Jesus Christ, in accord with the favor of his will, for the praise of the glory of his grace that he granted us in the beloved. In him we have redemption by his blood, the forgiveness of transgressions, in accord with the riches of his grace that he lavished upon us. In all wisdom and insight, he has made known to us the mystery of his will in accord with his favor that he set forth in him as a plan for the fullness of times, to sum up all things in Christ, in heaven and on earth. In him we were also chosen, destined in accord with the purpose of the one who accomplishes all things according to the intention of his will, so that we might exist for the praise of his glory, we who first hoped in Christ. In him you also, who have heard the word of truth, the gospel of your salvation, and have believed in him, were sealed with the promised Holy Spirit, which is the first installment of our inheritance toward redemption as God's possession, to the praise of his glory.

We have been adopted as children of God in order that we might show what grace can do in human beings. God has lavished this grace upon us in Jesus Christ so that we are redeemed and transformed. Now in us the Holy Spirit dwells. We have every possible spiritual blessing and can reveal to others the glories of the grace of God. Such is the calling of every Christian.

Chapter One

THE INNER PERSON

*B*efore we discuss how we may come to encounter the divine dwelling within, it will be important for us to consider and suggest answers to two preliminary questions. First, what picture should we keep before us of the inner nature of human beings? In this regard we are not interested in a modern psychological explanation of what constitutes a human being. Our quest is to find ways of discovering the divine indwelling based on an understanding of Scripture. Therefore it will be important for us to become familiar with how the inner person is described in Scripture. Second, if Scripture suggests that several parts make up the inner structure of human beings, can we present a model that will allow us to approach different passages of Scripture in a comprehensive way?

Sacred Scripture

The passages from the Old and New Testaments that mention the major commandments by which human beings are to live best illustrate the Scriptural view of the inner nature of human beings. Let us look then at three passages where these basic commandments are mentioned.

Hear, O Israel! The Lord is our God, the Lord alone! Therefore, you shall love the Lord, your God, with all your heart, and with all your soul, and with all your strength. (Dt 6:5)

One of the scribes, when he came forward and heard them disputing and saw how well he had answered them, asked him, "Which is the first of all the commandments?" Jesus replied, "The first is this: 'Hear, O Israel! The Lord our God is Lord alone! You shall love the Lord your God with all your heart, with all your soul, with all your mind, and with all your strength.' The second is this: 'You shall love your neighbor as yourself.' There is no other commandment greater than these." (Mk 12:28-31)

There was a scholar of the law who stood up to test him and said, "Teacher, what must I do to inherit eternal life?" Jesus said to him, "What is written in the law? How do you read it?" He said in reply, "You shall love the Lord, your God, with all your heart, with all your being, with all your strength, and with all your mind, and your neighbor as yourself." He replied to him, "You have answered correctly; do this and you will live." (Lk 10:25-28)

Deuteronomy mentions loving God with "heart," "soul," and "strength." Jesus in Matthew speaks of loving God with "heart," "soul," "mind," and "strength." The scholar in Luke refers to "heart," "being," "strength," and "mind." Thus we can summarize these passages: all three mention "heart" and "strength." Two speak of "mind." Two also speak of "soul." One passage mentions "being," which appears in the passage from Luke to take the place of "soul." Our four crucial words, therefore, are "heart," "soul," "mind," and "strength."

These passages describe how we are to love God. In each we see a description of what is considered the whole person. We can suppose that the reference to "strength" sums up our physical being, our inner vitality with which we are to "love" God. The other three terms, "heart," "soul," and "mind" describe the inner nature of human beings.

To these three terms we can add another that appears frequently in passages of Scripture to indicate the inner part of human beings: "spirit." It is in heart, soul, mind, and spirit, in different ways, that we find references in passages of Scripture to God abiding in human beings.

Let us become familiar with these terms, "heart," "soul," "mind," and "spirit," as they occur in Scripture.

Heart

What do we hear about the "heart" in Scripture? First, we learn (1 S 16:7):

> Not as man sees does God see, because man sees the appearance but the Lord looks into the heart.

God "observes" all human hearts.[1] He also "probes," "searches," and "tests" them.[2] What delights us is that God wants our hearts! Hosea tells us that God wishes us to return to him (2:26): "So I will allure her and speak to her heart." In Pr 23:36 God asks us "to give" him our hearts.

---

[1]   See Ws 1:6; Si 42:18; 2 Ch 6:30; Ps 44:22.
[2]   1 Ch 28:9, 29:17; Jr 17:10-12; Ps 17:3, 26:2, 139:23.

Our hearts, sadly, can turn to evil.[3] Jeremiah says of the human heart (17:9): "More tortuous than anything is the human heart, who can understand it?" Jesus is astonished at what "hardness" the human heart can show.[4] He lists many evils that can come forth from the human heart.[5] Jesus points out the importance of the heart when he tells us: "where your treasure is, there is your heart also."[6] His advice is that our hearts should be set on God. Most of all, it is important for human beings to lose their "hearts of stone," as Ezekiel describes in saying what God intends to do (11:19):[7]

> I will give them a new heart and put a new spirit within
> them; I will remove the stony heart from their bodies,
> and replace it with a natural heart, so that they will
> live according to my statutes, and observe and carry
> out my ordinances; thus they shall be my people and
> I will be their God.

Our hearts in their "natural" state are ones that will love and serve God.

Scripture passages tell us how human beings are to use their hearts. First and foremost as we heard in the passages quoted above, we are to "love" God with "all our heart."[8] We are also to "return" to him with our whole heart, [9] "search" for him,[10] "serve" him, [11] "trust" him,[12] and "worship" him[13] in the same way. Sol-

---

[3] See Gn 6:5, 8:21; Ps 36:2.
[4] Mk 3:5, 16:14.
[5] Mt 15:18-19; Lk 6:45.
[6] Mt 6:21; Lk 12:34.
[7] See also Ezk 36:26-27.
[8] See also Dt 13:4, 30:6; 2 K 23:25.
[9] Dt 30:10; 2 Ch 6:38; 1 S 7:3.
[10] Dt 4:29; Jr 29:13.
[11] Dt 10:12, 11:13; Jos 22:5; 1 Ch 28:9.
[12] Pr 3:5.
[13] 1 S 12:20, 12:24; 1 K 8:23; 2 M 1:3.

omon teaches us the type of heart we should desire (1 K 3:9-12):[14]

> "Give your servant, therefore, an understanding heart to judge your people and to distinguish right from wrong. For who is able to govern this vast people of yours?" The Lord was pleased that Solomon made this request. So God said to him: "Because you have asked for this—not for a long life for yourself, nor for riches, nor for the life of your enemies, but for understanding so that you may know what is right—I do as you requested. I give you a heart so wise and understanding that there has never been anyone like you up to now, and after you there will appear no one to equal you."

"Understanding" is what we should most desire in our hearts, so that we can know the ways of God. In the beautiful Psalm 119 where appeals of many kinds are made to God for a growth in holiness, the "heart" is frequently mentioned as central with its activity, as, for example, in the following verses (7-11):

> I will praise you with sincere heart as I study your
> just edicts.
> I will keep your laws; do not leave me all alone.
> How can the young walk without fault?
> Only by keeping your words.
> With all my heart I seek you; do not let me stray
> from your commands.
> In my heart I treasure your promise,
> so that I may not sin against you.

---

[14]   See also 2 Ch 9:23.

Jesus tells us the most perfect state of the heart (Mt 5:8): "Blessed are the pure of heart, for they shall see God."

If human beings strive to love God with all their heart, wonderful things happen. God tells Jeremiah how he will treat his people (24:6-7):

> I will look after them for their good, and bring them back to this land, to build them up, not to tear them down; to plant them, not to pluck them out. I will give them a heart with which to understand that I am the Lord. They shall be my people and I will be their God, for they shall return to me with their whole heart.

We learn that wisdom longs to dwell in the human heart but that she will test the person first (Si 4:16-18):

> If one trusts her, he will possess her; his descendants too will inherit her. She walks with him as a stranger, and at first she puts him to the test. Fear and dread she brings upon him and tries him with her discipline. With her precepts she puts him to the proof, until his heart is fully with her. Then she comes back to bring him happiness and reveal her secrets to him.

Jeremiah vividly describes how irresistible the word of God proved to be when it filled his heart (20:9):

> The word of the Lord has brought me derision and reproach all the day. I say to myself, I will not mention him, I will speak in his name no more But then it becomes like fire burning in my heart, imprisoned in my bones; I grow weary holding it in, I cannot endure it.

The word of God is like "fire burning" in the heart. It will burst forth in expression. St. Paul speaks too of the word of God being in the heart (Rm 8:8-10):

> "The word is near you, in your mouth and in your heart"
> (that is, the word of faith that we preach),
> for, if you confess with your mouth that Jesus is Lord
> and believe in your heart that God raised him from the
> dead, you will be saved.

Our heart is to be the seat of our belief. St. Paul also tells us how to serve Jesus (Col 3:23): "Whatever you do, do from the heart, as for the Lord and not for others." In Jesus we also see the ideal of the human heart, for he says to us (Mt 11:29): "I am meek and humble of heart."

Soul

Let us now look at what Scripture tells us about the "soul." First, we learn that this soul is adversely affected by the body in which it dwells (Ws 9:13-18):

> For what person knows God's counsel, or who can
> conceive what our Lord intends? For the deliberations
> of mortals are timid, and unsure are our plans. For
> the corruptible body burdens the soul and the earthen
> shelter weighs down the mind that has many con-
> cerns. And scarce do we guess the things on earth, and
> what is within our grasp we find with difficulty; but
> when things are in heaven, who can search them out?
> Or who ever knew your counsel, except you had given
> Wisdom and sent your Holy Spirit from on high? And
> thus were the paths of those on earth made straight,

and mortals learned what was your pleasure, and were
saved by Wisdom.

The body "burdens" the soul and "weighs down" the mind that is
filled with cares. It is beyond the soul and mind of human beings
to grasp divine matters and it is only God's gift of Wisdom and
the Holy Spirit that teaches them. Elsewhere we hear of the soul
being "weary" (Jr 31:25). Jesus in Gethsemane says of his soul:
"My soul is sorrowful even to death" (Mt 26:38; Mk 14:34).

In relation to God we find the soul described as "waiting"
for the Lord (Ps 33:20); "longing," "thirsting," and "yearning"
for God.[15] We learn that the soul should "rest" only in God (Ps
62:2, 6). "Happy" is the soul if it "fears the Lord" (Si 34:15).
Isaiah describes what God does for the soul (Is 61:10):

> I rejoice heartily in the Lord, in my God is the joy
> of my soul. For he has clothed me with a robe of sal-
> vation, and wrapped me in a mantle of justice, like
> a bridegroom adorned with a diadem, like a bride
> bedecked with her jewels.

God is the "joy" of the soul to which he brings salvation and
justice. Thus God is also called "the portion of the soul" (Lm
3:24).

What is the soul in human beings to do? We find it mentioned with "heart" in the exhortations mentioned above to
"love,"[16] "return to,"[17] "search for,"[18] and "serve"[19] God with all
"heart and soul." Elsewhere we hear of other activities recom-
mended for the soul. It is to "bless the Lord."[20] It is also to "revere"

---

[15]   Is 26:9; Ps 42:2, 63:2, 84:3, 130:6.
[16]   Dt 13:4; 30:6; 2 K 23:25.
[17]   Dt 30:10; 2 Ch 6:38.
[18]   Dt 4:29.
[19]   Dt 10:12, 11:13; Jos 22:5; 1 Ch 28:9.
[20]   Ps 103:1-2, 22, 104:1, 35.

the Lord.[21] In Psalm 131 we learn how best to keep one's "heart" and "soul" in the presence of God:

> Lord, my heart is not proud; nor are my eyes haughty.
> I do not busy myself with great matters,
> with things too sublime for me.
> Rather, I have stilled my soul,
> hushed it like a weaned child.
> Like a weaned child on its mother's lap,
> so is my soul within me.
> Israel, hope in the Lord, now and forever.

We are to be lowly of heart and keep our soul "still" as we pray. When heart and soul are thus, then we can see clearly that we should place all our hope in God. Mary also teaches us what to do with our "soul" and "spirit" (Lk 1:46):

> And Mary said: "My soul proclaims the greatness of the Lord; my spirit rejoices in God my savior."

The soul of Mary, who had just been chosen to be the mother of the Messiah, blesses God for his wondrous works, choosing, as he had, a lowly and humble maiden for an honor beyond all description.

Mind

What does Scripture tell us about the human mind? First, as quoted above from Wisdom 9:13-18, we hear that, like the soul, it is hindered by the body and has itself "many concerns." Wisdom 4:12 tells us how vulnerable the mind is:

---

[21] Si 7:29.

> For the witchery of paltry things obscures what is right
> and the whirl of desire transforms the innocent mind.

Desire captivates the mind and leads it into wrong doing.

Scripture also describes the mind as the place where human beings form their plans but it is God who decides the course of events (Pr 16:9):

> In their minds people plan their course but the Lord directs their steps.

All human conduct derives from the mind (Si 37:17):

> Most important of all, pray to God to set your feet in the path of truth.
> A word is the source of every deed; a thought, of every act.
>
> The root of all conduct is the mind; four branches it shoots forth:
> Good and evil, death and life, their absolute mistress is the tongue.

The mind thinks; the tongue speaks. From the mind come "four branches" that lead to "good and evil, death and life." What the mind chooses the mouth manifests. How powerful, therefore, is the mind! How important it is for it to receive from God the "path of truth." Fortunately, it can. Proverbs 18:15 tells us:

> The mind of the intelligent gains knowledge and the ear of the wise seeks knowledge.

The mind can receive "knowledge." "Wisdom" likewise can come to the mind (Si 51:25-26):

I open my mouth and speak of [wisdom]:
gain, at no cost, wisdom for yourselves.
Submit your neck to her yoke,
 that your mind may accept her teaching.
For she is close to those who seek her,
and the one who is in earnest finds her.

Scripture teaches us that God "searches" and "probes" the mind.[22] He also "enlightens" it (Si 6:37). St. Peter tells us to take charge of our minds (1 P 1:13). St. Paul urges us (Rm 12:2):

Do not conform yourselves to this age but be transformed by the renewal of your mind, that you may discern what is the will of God, what is good and pleasing and perfect.

Our minds are to be renewed by grace which will allow us to think correctly, discerning then "the will of God." St. Paul elsewhere tells us that Christians possess a magnificent gift (1 Cor 2:16):

We have not received the spirit of the world but the Spirit that is from God, so that we may understand the things freely given us by God. And we speak about them not with words taught by human wisdom, but with words taught by the Spirit, describing spiritual realities in spiritual terms. Now natural persons do not accept what pertains to the Spirit of God, for to them it is foolishness, and they cannot understand it, because it is judged spiritually. The spiritual person, however, can judge everything but is not subject to judgment by anyone. For "who has known the mind of the Lord, so as to counsel him?" But we have the mind of Christ.

---

[22]   Jr 11:20, 17:10, 20:12; Ps 26:2.

By the gift of the Holy Spirit, our minds no longer view things in a "natural" way but in a "spiritual" way. Our minds are truly transformed within and, as Christ thinks, so we come to think.

Spirit

In addition to the terms "heart," "soul," and "mind," we find in Scripture frequent references to the "spirit" of human beings as both their very life and also their inner nature. It is the "spirit within that gives life."[23] When the "spirit" departs, a person dies.[24] As a seat of inner life the spirit is described in Scripture in various ways. It can be "steadfast" (Ps 51:12), "willing" (Ps 51:14), "strong" (Ps 138:3; Lk 1:80), "humble" (Pr 23:23), "contented" (Si 30:5); "generous" (Si 35:7), "joyous" (Tb 13:7; Si 35:8) and "fervent" (Rm 12:14). Jesus calls those "poor in spirit" "blessed" (Mt 5:3). He states that the "spirit is willing but the flesh is weak" (Mt 26:41; Mk 14:38).

The spirit can also be "crushed" (Ps 34:19; Is 57:15), "broken" (Ps 51:19), "faint" (Ps 77:4, 142:4), and "embittered" (Ps 106:33). Job describes how he suffers in his spirit.[25] Jesus too, on one occasion, sighed "from the depth of his spirit" (Mk 8:12).

The spirit is associated with "understanding" (Si 39:6) and "wisdom" (Eph 1:17). Job says of the spirit: "it is a spirit in a person, the breath of the Almighty that gives understanding" (32:8). Jesus suggests the importance of the spirit when he tells the woman of Samaria that people one day "will worship in spirit and truth" (Jn 4:23). St. Paul speaks of "serving" with the spirit (Rm 1:9) and "praying with spirit and mind" (1 Cor 14:15).

In Ezekiel, spirit is mentioned with heart when God speaks

---

[23] Is 42:5; Ws 15:11, 15:16; Ezk 37:1-10; Zc 12:1.
[24] Ps 31:6; Ws 2:3, 16:14; Mt 27:50; Jn 19:30.
[25] Job 6:4, 7:11, 17:1.

of giving human beings "a new heart and a new spirit."[26] In other passages of Scripture we find spirit linked with soul. Isaiah says: "My soul yearns for you in the night; yes, my spirit keeps vigil for you" (26:9). Mary sings with delight: "My soul proclaims the greatness of the Lord; my spirit rejoices in God my savior" (Lk 1:47). St. Paul prays: "may you entirely, soul, spirit and body, be preserved blameless for the coming of our Lord Jesus Christ" (1 Th 5:23). In Heb 4:12 we hear about the word of God:

> Indeed, the word of God is living and effective, sharper than any two-edged sword, penetrating even between soul and spirit, joints and marrow, and able to discern reflections and thoughts of the heart.

References to "spirit" closely resemble those to "soul" yet somehow they seem also to be distinct. Both are clearly the seats of the deepest feelings of a person. With them someone often responds to the actions of God.

Model of the Inner Person: the Will

In the words "heart," "mind," "soul" and "spirit" in Scripture we can clearly find designations of the inner life of human beings. These terms may not exclusively or comprehensively designate this inner life as portrayed in Scripture but they are the most common terms that do so. Can we now suggest a model that will allow us to approach different passages of Scripture mentioning these parts of the inner nature of a person in a comprehensive way? In the Introduction we discussed the calling of each Christian. We suggested that this call involves our surrendering our

---

[26] Ezk 11:19, 36:26-27, 37:14, 39:29.

wills to Jesus, allowing him to dwell in his Spirit in our hearts. If we do this, the life of God will fill our souls and we will radiate this life to others.

Now in order to help us in our journey to God within I would like gradually to build a model concerning the inner nature of human beings. The basic component of this model will be the human will, free to choose and to act at each moment. We will sum up the powers of the will in the words that Scripture has given us: "heart," "mind," "soul" and "spirit." In this proposed model, "heart" will include all the emotions that we can freely express. "Mind" will include all intellectual activity. "Soul" and "spirit" will include the whole range of our psychological being, including activities of the heart, mind, memory, and imagination. These two words point to the most intimate and essential parts of a human person. With this model, we will see that sometimes the words "heart," "mind," "soul" and "spirit" will express the will itself. At other times they will point to aspects of the will, the will itself being greater than they and essentially distinct from them.

Our model up to this point is that of a will that expresses itself in "heart," "mind," "soul" and "spirit." We now further suggest (as discussed in the Introduction) that the will has one essential freedom: it can choose to love. The great commandments of the Old and New Testaments urge human beings to use their wills to "love God with all their heart, soul, mind, and strength, and to love their neighbors as themselves." The model, therefore, that we offer thus far is that of a human will capable of using all its powers, "heart," "mind," "soul" and "spirit," to love God and neighbor.

Optimal Functioning of the Will

Let us look more closely at the human will. Does Scripture tell us anywhere of its optimal functioning? One passage from Scripture that well illuminates such a functioning is Proverbs 2:1-11:

> My child, if you receive my words and treasure
>   my commands,
> Turning your ear to wisdom, inclining your heart
>   to understanding;
> Yes, if you call to intelligence, and to understanding
>   raise your voice;
> If you seek her like silver, and like hidden treasures
>   search her out:
> Then will you understand the fear of the Lord;
>   the knowledge of God you will find;
> For the Lord gives wisdom, from his mouth come
>   knowledge and understanding;
> He has counsel in store for the upright;
>   he is the shield of those who walk honestly,
> Guarding the paths of justice,
>   protecting the way of his pious ones.
> Then you will understand rectitude and justice,
>   honesty, every good path;
> For wisdom will enter your heart, knowledge will
>   please your soul,
> Discretion will watch over you, understanding
>   will guard you.

In this amazing passage we can discern a pattern for the relationship of our will and the action of God. The following tables lay out what this passage says about the actions of our wills and the actions of God.

ACTIONS OF THE HUMAN WILL

Activity	Verse
Receive words	1
Treasure commands	1
Turn ear to wisdom	2
Incline heart to understanding	2
Call to intelligence	3
Raise voice to understanding	3
Seek understanding like silver	4
Search for understanding like treasure	4

ACTIONS OF GOD

Activity	Verse
Gives wisdom	6
From his mouth comes knowledge and understanding	6
Has counsel for the upright	7
Is the shield for those who walk honestly	7
Guards the paths of justice	8
Protects the way of his pious ones	8

This passage also states clearly what happens when we turn our wills to God and his teachings. Addressing the listener as "you," the writer of Proverbs describes these consequences.

CONSEQUENCES FOR THE PERSON

Activity	Verse
You will understand the fear of the Lord	5
You will find the knowledge of God	5
You will understand rectitude and justice, honesty, every good path	9

REASONS FOR THESE CONSEQUENCES

Activity	Verse
Wisdom will enter your heart	10
Knowledge will please your soul	10
Discretion will watch over you	11
Understanding will guard you	11

We can summarize this passage as follows. If a person by acts of the will (1-4) turns full attention to holy teachings, then that person, through the kindness of God, will be filled with knowledge of God (5), wisdom (6, 10), knowledge (6, 10), understanding (6,11), counsel (7), and discretion (11). What we see is a process of attention of the will, attended by a consequent outpouring by God of truly valuable gifts that then fill the person. This passage in Proverbs mentions some of the gifts that have been traditionally associated with the Holy Spirit: wisdom, knowledge, understanding, counsel, and fear of the Lord.

In its list of gifts this passage calls to mind the description of the Messiah that Isaiah gives (11:1-3):

But a shoot shall sprout from the stump of Jesse,
and from his roots a bud shall blossom.

The spirit of the Lord shall rest upon him:
a spirit of wisdom and of understanding,
a spirit of counsel and of strength,
a spirit of knowledge and of fear of the Lord,
and his delight shall be the fear of the Lord.

Isaiah lists the gifts that rested upon Jesus, who was filled with wisdom, understanding, counsel, strength, knowledge, and fear of the Lord. The last verse suggests an aspect of the will of Jesus: his delight was to focus upon God.

The passage from Proverbs shows us the freedom that we have. We can turn our full attention to God and, when we do in complete trust, we will find ourselves filled with divine gifts. God wants to bless us in this way. The choice to receive these blessings remains entirely ours. Our will is free to choose.

Common Functioning of the Will

Why, we may ask, does the human will not always function perfectly? Why does a person who believes in God not simply yield to divine grace on each occasion and become filled with divine blessings? The long history of the human race has made very clear that such perfect submission to the action of the divine is rare. Why is this so? The story of Adam and Eve (discussed above in the Introduction) gives clear answers to these questions. Our human parents found something very attractive, indeed irresistible, in the fruit of the tree that they were told not to eat. They showed themselves quite capable of forgetting God and his commands and of being able, trusting in their judgment and desires, to make a choice that would have far-reaching consequences. What we can say is that their wills forgot God and heeded only self. We are all children of these parents and our wills easily turn aside from God.

It is self in all of us that prevents our perfect response to God and to the gifts he offers. Where does this self abide? As part of our model, we suggest that it resides in the will. What happens from childhood is that our self develops moment by moment. Slowly but surely it fills our wills as we come to establish our particular likes and dislikes, our mental strengths, our emotional range, our body of knowledge, our memories, our flights of imagination, and our religious beliefs and practices. What is described here, of course, is the development of the personality of an individual. It is clearly part of the destiny of each person that such a self emerge over the years. The spiritual challenge, however, is to ensure that this self can be surrendered to the workings of divine grace. This challenge is a serious one. Why?

Once self fills the will, it yields with great difficulty. The will becomes accustomed to nurturing this self. The will comes to trust and to sustain this self. Why should it not? This self usually has many good features. It is attractive and grows more so as a person learns more, responds more to the beauties of the world, and develops all given talents. Slowly, silently this self comes to dominate the will. As it does so, the will gradually loses its freedom to surrender totally to grace.

What words we find to describe a condition in which self dominates too greatly! Self-centered, self-opinionated, self-willed! Self-conceit, self-indulgence, self-love! How difficult we find it to sacrifice our different selves! The successful self. The brilliant self. The witty self. The wealthy self. The physically-fit self. The injured self. The insulted self. The forgotten self. The religious self with its views of the holy.

Is it necessary, we may ask, to empty our wills of such selves? All of us know that we can fail to make any concerted effort to do so. We can live in an easy state of compromise in which we to some extent love God and others but continue at the same time to love and admire ourselves. Here, however, we must face an essential truth: if we consistently nurture and cultivate self, we shall not discover the divine indwelling in our souls. This is the price we shall pay for our compromise.

In all three Gospels we hear Jesus say: "If anyone wishes to come after me, he must deny himself and take up his cross and follow me" (Mk 8:34).[27] In his reference Luke tells us that this self-denial is to be a "daily" occurrence. At Mt 10.38 Jesus says: "whoever does not take up his cross and follow after me is not worthy of me." To be a disciple of Jesus will involve conscious choices that may be difficult. To be worthy of him, we must "take up our cross." We must also "deny" ourselves. We suggest that such denial involves resistance to the self that has come to dominate our wills.

If, as we suggested in the Introduction, we are truly called to be transformed into the image of Jesus, we have to learn to surrender our wills in perfect obedience to him. This surrender is one to Jesus dwelling at the center of our very being. It is only, we suggest further, a will that has become empty of self and of self-will that can make such a surrender. Learning how to empty our wills of self becomes an essential part of our journey to discover the divine indwelling.

We can now add further details to the model we propose to use in the chapters to come. The major feature of human beings is that we have free will.

- This will has powers summed up in the terms "heart," "mind," "soul" and "spirit."
- This will can choose to love both God and neighbor.
- This will can be full of self and pursue the interests of self.
- This will can be empty of self and surrender to the workings of grace within.

---

[27] Cf. Mt 16:24 and Lk 9:23.

Our conviction is that human beings are invited not only to discover God within but also to enter into a relationship of love with him there.

We shall now suggest various steps by which the will can become empty and learn to surrender to the divine indwelling. For every step we will make the riches of Scripture our guide. We shall move forward slowly and exactly, bearing in mind always, of course, that the spiritual journey of each person differs and unfolds according to the workings of God's grace. In no way are we suggesting that the steps we describe can be followed in order, one by one. Our aim is rather to lay out the principal elements of a relationship with God abiding in the center of our being. Teresa of Avila in her great work on prayer, *The Interior Castle*, describes the journey to God at the center of the soul in terms of the image of a castle of crystal with many mansions within and many roads to the most important seventh mansions.[28] In her use of this image Teresa emphasizes that the route to God can take place in many, many ways with different paths through the mansions being possible. What she does is to lay out in great detail the setting where such a journey may take place. In a similar way we shall set out the landscape for the discovery of God within our being, clarifying what appear to be necessary aspects of the journey. For each person God will lay out the specific journey to be traveled. Such is the mystery and the wonder of the working of divine grace.

---

[28] *The Collected Works of St. Teresa of Avila*, trans. K. Kavanaugh, OCD and O. Rodriguez, OCD (Washington, DC: ICS Publications, 1987), 2nd ed., Volume 2.

Chapter Two

REMEMBERING AND FORGETTING

As we begin our journey to the discovery of God within, let us sum up our picture of human beings. Sirach 17:1-13 does this admirably for us:

> The Lord from the earth created human beings,
> and in his own image he made them.
> Limited days of life he gives them
> and makes them return to earth again.
> He endows human beings with a strength of his own,
> and with power over all things else on earth.
> He puts the fear of them in all flesh,
> and gives them rule over beasts and birds.
> He forms their tongues and eyes and ears,
> and imparts to them an understanding heart.
> With wisdom and knowledge he fills them;
> good and evil he shows them.
> He looks with favor upon their hearts,
> and shows them his glorious works,
> That they may describe the wonders of his deeds
> and praise his holy name.
> He has set before them knowledge,
> a law of life as their inheritance;

An everlasting covenant he has made with them,
his commandments he has revealed to them.
His majestic glory their eyes beheld,
his glorious voice their ears heard.
He says to them, "Avoid all evil";
To each of them he gives precepts about their neighbors.
Their ways are ever known to him;
they cannot be hidden from his eyes.

We learn that God has given us "strength." He has given us "an understanding heart."

He has filled us "with wisdom and knowledge." It is he who shows us what is "good and evil." God's purpose is that we may understand his "deeds" and "praise his holy name."

He has given human beings a "law" in an "everlasting covenant." He has revealed to us "commandments" to obey. We are to "avoid all evil." We are called into a relationship with our neighbors. All of our actions lie open to God.

God has made us to be free, free to love and to serve him, free to acknowledge his wonder and glory. In this chapter we will focus on one aspect of that freedom of will: our capacity to remember and to forget. Let us consider these two powers of the will for a moment. A brief exercise will prove helpful. First, let us make two brief lists, a page each, containing three columns entitled 'People," "Events," and "Things." On the first page, let us fill in each column with what we rejoice to remember from our own lives. Then, on the second page, let us fill in each column with what we would prefer to forget. Now, and this is crucial for us to notice, let us realize that the specific items are not important. What is important is that we possess the capacity to remember and to forget. It is not the case that we are slaves, that we have to remember certain things and cannot forget others. No, we have the power to remember and to forget. This power is a crucial feature of free will. Perhaps, in the case of forgetting, there is much pain and sorrow associated with this activity. But we can forget. If negative memories are troubling us, we have the capacity to stop and to turn our thoughts in another direction. We can choose to remember something while we forget what is bothering us. This capacity of the will is essential in our search to find God within.

In this regard it is helpful to recall what God said to Cain when his offering was not accepted. We do not know what the trouble with his offering was but clearly, since we are not given the details, it is unimportant in the story. What we are to heed carefully is what God tells Cain (Gn 4:3-7)[1]:

> In the course of time Cain brought an offering to the Lord from the fruit of the soil, while Abel, for his part, brought one of the best firstlings of his flock. The Lord looked with favor on Abel and his offering, but on Cain and his offering he did not. Cain greatly resented this and was crestfallen. So the Lord said to Cain: "Why are you so resentful and crestfallen? If you do well, you can hold up your head; but if not, sin is a demon lurking at the door: his urge is toward you, yet you can be his master."

This passage presents an essential truth. We can choose our actions and we can "do well." Even though sin "lurks at our door," we can be its "master." Sadly Cain chose to act in an evil way but, even though he did so, he had the freedom to act in the opposite way. In a similar manner we always possess the freedom to use our wills either to remember or to forget.

---

[1]   A profound treatment of this passage is to be found in John Steinbeck's novel *East of Eden*, first published in 1952.

First of all, then, what are we to remember? The Old Testament urges people to remember God.[2] We are to recall his commandments[3] and his works.[4] Our freedom to do so accords with the gifts God has given us (Si 15:14-19):

> When God, in the beginning, created human beings,
> he made them subject to their own free choice.
> If you choose, you can keep the commandments;
> it is loyalty to do his will.
> There are set before you fire and water;
> to whichever you choose, stretch forth your hand.
> Before human beings are life and death,
> whichever they choose shall be given to them.
> Immense is the wisdom of the Lord;
> he is mighty in power, and all-seeing.
> The eyes of God see all he has made;
> he understands every deed of human beings.

We have the freedom to remember the "commandments." Choosing to obey them will bring us "life." This choice of remembering God and his commandments is something we are to do from our earliest days: "Remember your creator in the days of your youth" (Ec 12:1). Remembering God will bring us much joy. At Isaiah 48:17-18 God says:

> Thus says the Lord, your redeemer,
> the Holy One of Israel:

---

[2] See, e.g., Dt 8:18; 2 S 14:11; Ps 42:7; 119:55; 137:6; Jr 51:50; Ezk 6:9; Zc 10:9.

[3] See e.g., Ex 15:26, 20:6; Lv 22:31, 26:3; Nb 15:40; Dt 5:10, 6:17, 7:11, 8:2; Jos 22:5; 1 K 3:14; 1 Ch 28:8; Ne 1:5, 10:30; Si 1:23, 28:7, 37:12; Ml 3:22.

[4] Tb 12:7, 12:11; Jb 36:24, 37:14; Ps 46:9, 66:5, 71:16, 73:28, 77:13, 78:7, 107:22, 111:2, 143:5, 145:4; Si 42:15.

"I, the Lord, your God,
teach you what is for your good,
and lead you on the way you should go.
If you would hearken to my commandments,
your prosperity would be like a river,
and your vindication like the waves of the sea."

In the New Testament we are exhorted to remember the teachings of Jesus and the apostles. Jesus tells us that the role of the Holy Spirit will be to remind us of all that Jesus taught (Jn 14:16-27):

> The Advocate, the Holy Spirit whom the Father will send in my name — he will teach you everything and remind you of all that I told you. Peace I leave with you; my peace I give to you. Not as the world gives do I give it to you. Do not let your hearts be troubled or afraid.

The Holy Spirit stirs up our memories so that, like the apostles, we can remember what Jesus teaches us. In a similar vein Peter considers it an important role for him to remind the followers of Jesus of what he has been teaching (2 P 1:12-15):

> Therefore, I will always remind you of these things, even though you already know them and are established in the truth you have.
>
> I think it right, as long as I am in this "tent," to stir you up by a reminder, since I know that I will soon have to put it aside, as indeed our Lord Jesus Christ has shown me. I shall also make every effort to enable you always to remember these things after my departure.

He says further (2 P 3:1):

> This is now, beloved, the second letter I am writing to you; through these letters, by way of reminder, I am trying to stir up your sincere disposition, to recall the words previously spoken by the holy prophets and the commandment of the Lord and Savior through your apostles.

Likewise, Paul urges Timothy: "remember Jesus Christ, raised from the dead, a descendant of David" (2 Tm 2:8). At Acts 20:35 the exhortation is given: "Keep in mind the words of the Lord Jesus who himself said, 'It is more blessed to give than to receive.'" Likewise, at Jude 17, we hear: "But you, beloved, remember the words spoken beforehand by the apostles of our Lord Jesus Christ, for they told you, 'In the last time there will be scoffers who will live according to their own godless desires.'"

In the New Testament there is one act of remembering that is to be central to our lives. At the Last Supper Jesus says: "This is my body, which will be given for you; do this in memory of me" (Lk 22:19). We find a similar exhortation in Paul's description of the Last Supper (1 Cor 11:23-25):

> For I received from the Lord what I also handed on to you, that the Lord Jesus, on the night he was handed over, took bread, and, after he had given thanks, broke it and said, "This is my body that is for you. Do this in remembrance of me." In the same way also the cup, after supper, saying, "This cup is the new covenant in my blood. Do this, as often as you drink it, in remembrance of me."

All these passages considered thus far teach us important truths.

We are human beings endowed with free will. We can use that free will to choose to believe in God, to accept and honor his commandments, and to praise his works. As Christians, we are to remember in particular the words and works of Jesus Christ and to remember him especially in the "breaking of the bread," the Eucharist. The major act of our wills, therefore, is to remember. As we make a decision to use our wills in this way, we can also consciously choose to forget whatever in our past may hinder this choice. Wondrously, we discover in Scripture God urging us to do this very thing (Is 43:18-19):

> Remember not the events of the past, the things of long ago consider not. See, I am doing something new! Now it springs forth, do you not perceive it? In the desert I make a way, in the wasteland, rivers.

Paul gives a splendid example of someone who took this advice. He had persecuted the followers of Jesus and had approved of the murder of Stephen. Yet, more than any of the apostles, he brought the good news to the Gentiles. He says explicitly that he chooses to forget and to remember instead what he is working for and for whom (Ph 3:13-14):

> Just one thing: forgetting what lies behind but straining forward to what lies ahead, I continue my pursuit toward the goal, the prize of God's upward calling, in Christ Jesus.

Let us now look more intently at the capacity of remembering and forgetting in our journey to discover the divine indwelling. If we are to come to encounter God within and to abide in the divine presence, our first task will be to learn constantly to remember God. We can do so because we have free will but it

45

requires practice for us to make such remembrance a way of life. We all know how easily we can become distracted. Our minds flit here and there. Our emotions shift from positive to negative. Often our souls seem much too full of the world and its concerns. How are we to learn serenely to gaze at God within? Our first task will be to discern clearly the temptations that will keep us from doing so. Let us look at those which Jesus endured.

Matthew describes the first of the temptations of Jesus as follows (4:1-4):

> Then Jesus was led by the Spirit into the desert to be tempted by the Devil. He fasted for forty days and forty nights, and afterwards he was hungry. The tempter approached and said to him, "If you are the Son of God, command that these stones become loaves of bread." He said in reply, "It is written: 'One does not live by bread alone, but by every word that comes forth from the mouth of God.'"

After his long period of fasting and prayer, Jesus is hungry. How does the Devil tempt him? First, he draws Jesus to focus upon himself and his needs. He then attempts to sow doubt into Jesus' mind about his identity: "If you are the Son of God." His method, therefore, is to urge Jesus to remember himself and his personal needs. He further tempts Jesus to prove his divine identity to himself by performing a miracle for himself. He hopes that Jesus will, for a moment, step outside the incarnation and forget his identity as "Son of Man." But Jesus resists the temptation, perfectly using his free will. He forgets himself and his immediate needs. He remembers Scripture and its teaching that the true food for human beings is "every word that comes forth from the mouth of God."

In light of the full message of the Gospel what amazing

riches are to be found in this first temptation! First, with regard to the response that Jesus gives to the Devil, we can ponder the great mystery that the opening of John's Gospel describes (1:1-5):

> In the beginning was the Word,
> and the Word was with God,
> and the Word was God.
> He was in the beginning with God.
> All things came to be through him,
> and without him nothing came to be.
> What came to be through him was life,
> and this life was the light of the human race;
> the light shines in the darkness,
> and the darkness has not overcome it.

Jesus says that human beings live "by every word that comes from the mouth of God." John has taught us that Jesus is this very Word. Truly it is he who is "the Alpha and the Omega, the first and the last, the beginning and the end" (Rv 22:13). Paul brilliantly describes who Jesus is (Col 1:15-20):

> He is the image of the invisible God, the firstborn of all creation. For in him were created all things in heaven and on earth, the visible and the invisible, whether thrones or dominions or principalities or powers; all things were created through him and for him. He is before all things, and in him all things hold together. He is the head of the body, the church. He is the beginning, the firstborn from the dead, that in all things he himself might be preeminent. For in him all the fullness of God was pleased to dwell, and through him to reconcile all things for him, making peace by the blood of his cross through him, whether those on earth or those in heaven.

In Jesus "all the fullness of God" dwells. He is the Word of God who has taken flesh for our sakes. In his incarnation as "Son of Man," the Devil tempts him to use his powers as Word of God for himself. Jesus refuses. He resists this temptation entirely and shows himself to be the perfect human being, obedient in his human nature to "every word that comes from the mouth of God." He teaches us likewise always to remember first the teachings of God before any claims to what may enhance our own position.

Second, Jesus is tempted to make bread to satisfy his own hunger. He resists this attempt of the Devil to make him use his divine powers for himself. Later in his life, it is true, Jesus will use his divine powers to transform one natural substance into another. He will transform bread into his own body and feed his people at each celebration of the Eucharist. Thus Jesus says of himself (Jn 6:51):

> I am the living bread that came down from heaven;
> whoever eats this bread will live forever; and the bread
> that I will give is my flesh for the life of the world.

Jesus makes the "bread of life" for us out of ordinary bread but, however hungry he was, he would not make bread for himself. When tempted to do so, he chose to forget himself and to remember God.

From the first temptation we learn that, like Jesus, we may often be tempted to remember ourselves in a situation and to make our needs of central importance. We may forget God altogether. But, like Jesus also, we have the freedom to forget ourselves and to remember Scripture and its teachings. Then, like Jesus, we shall be using our capacity for remembering and forgetting in a spiritual and perfect way.

The Devil tempted Jesus a second time (Mt 4:5-7):

Then the Devil took him to the holy city, and made
him stand on the parapet of the temple, and said to
him, "If you are the Son of God, throw yourself down.
For it is written: 'He will command his angels concerning you' and 'with their hands they will support
you, lest you dash your foot against a stone.'" Jesus
answered him, "Again it is written, 'You shall not put
the Lord, your God, to the test.'"

The Devil once again tempts Jesus to focus upon himself and to
prove his divine identity to himself by hurling himself into danger. Since Jesus in the first temptation had used Scripture as his
shield, the Devil now shamelessly even quotes Scripture to him,
referring to Psalm 91:11-12 where divine protection is promised.
Here again Jesus forgets himself and remembers the teachings
of Scripture about the appropriate behavior for human beings in
relation to God. The Devil tries to make Jesus forget his human
nature and prove to himself that he is "Son of God," but Jesus
remembers that God is not someone to be tested. God's promises
of divine protection were for those facing the troubles of life, not
for those trying to get God to act on their behalf in miraculous
ways. As in the first temptation, Jesus in this second temptation
perfectly uses his free will to forget himself and to remember
Scripture and its teachings.

A third time the Devil tempts Jesus (Mt 4:8-10):

Then the Devil took him up to a very high mountain,
and showed him all the kingdoms of the world in their
magnificence, and he said to him, "All these I shall
give to you, if you will prostrate yourself and worship
me." At this, Jesus said to him, "Get away, Satan! It is
written: 'The Lord, your God, shall you worship and
him alone shall you serve.'"

The Devil now shows Jesus what he imagines any person would wish: "all the kingdoms of the world in their magnificence." He offers the gift of these at the price of worship of himself. Once again, he tempts Jesus to remember only himself and to forget all else: the incarnation, his purpose for coming into the world, his love for his followers, his zeal to glorify his Father. Here again Jesus perfectly uses his free will: he forgets himself and remembers the teachings of Scripture that God alone is to be worshipped.

From this temptation we learn also a truth about human lives. Perhaps we see those who focus only upon "self," who work solely for their own advantage and the advantage of what sadly may be simply an extension of "self," family and particular friends, becoming rich and prosperous. Perhaps when we look at the lives of such people, it seems that no evil approaches them, no sorrow saddens their way. Perhaps we may even be tempted to ask why such people meet with unlimited success and unbounded good fortune. This third temptation of Jesus teaches us not to be surprised but, on the contrary, to expect that such will be the case.

St. Paul tells us that we shall reap as we sow (Gal 6:7-8):

> Make no mistake: God is not mocked, for a person will reap only what he sows, because the one who sows for his flesh will reap corruption from the flesh, but the one who sows for the spirit will reap eternal life from the spirit.

The Devil, it appears, chose to serve only himself and continues to do so. He therefore tempts human beings to do the same. If we choose to serve only "self," it may happen that our lives will come to reflect "all the kingdoms of the world in their magnificence." We may see this happening also in the lives of others. But the way of Jesus is different: it is the way of the cross, of self-sacrifice in the service of others. Remembering "self" may bring a harvest but it is entirely a mortal one. Jesus told us (Mt 7:13-14):

> Enter through the narrow gate; for the gate is wide
> and the road broad that leads to destruction, and those
> who enter through it are many. How narrow the gate
> and constricted the road that leads to life. And those
> who find it are few.

Only remembering God and the "narrow gate" will allow us to live in communion with God and especially with God present within our own being.

From the three temptations of Jesus, we can observe how we, like him, are endowed with free will that allows us in any situation to choose what to remember and what to forget. We learn that, with this capacity, our inclination should be to forget ourselves and to remember always God and his teachings. If we look and listen to Jesus in another situation, we see him once again showing us how to use our free will to remember and to forget.

Let us listen to Jesus as he speaks from the cross, as recorded by the writers of the Gospels. At Luke 23:34 Jesus says, as he is being crucified: "Father, forgive them. They know not what they are doing." At the most terrible point in his passion, Jesus asks his Father to overlook and to forget what human beings are doing to him. Jesus himself chooses to forgive and to forget. He calls on his Father in prayer, remembering the boundless mercy of God. Psalm 103 tells us of this mercy (8-14):

> Merciful and gracious is the Lord,
> slow to anger, abounding in kindness.
> God does not always rebuke
> and nurses no lasting anger.
> He has not dealt with us as our sins merit,
> nor requited us as our deeds deserve.
> As the heavens tower over the earth,

so God's love towers over the faithful.
As far as the east is from the west,
so far have our sins been removed from us.
As a father has compassion on his children
so the Lord has compassion on the faithful.
For he knows how we are formed;
he remembers that we are dust.

God forgives and forgets what we have done wrong. Jesus in his words to his Father teaches us ever to remember the compassion of God, ever to forgive and forget both our own sins and the sins of others.

At another point in the crucifixion, John describes Jesus' words to Mary (19:26-27):

> When Jesus saw his mother and the disciple there whom he loved, he said to his mother, "Woman, behold, your son." Then he said to the disciple, "Behold, your mother." And from that hour the disciple took her into his home.

Jesus bids Mary henceforth to consider John as her son, and he, Mary as his mother. This exhortation to Mary has traditionally been seen to have a more far-reaching meaning than the new relationship between Mary and John. The disciple John represents all Christians. Mary is to be mother of all Christians who are to view her as having this role. From the cross Jesus summons Mary to "remember" John, to see him as her son and to love him as she did her own son. John, like every Christian, is to "remember" Mary, to hold her in deep affection and high regard as "mother." In these words of Jesus we see a most valuable and precious call to us to use our wills to remember in a specific way.

At Luke 23:39-43 we learn of the encounter of Jesus with those who were crucified with him:

> Now one of the criminals hanging there reviled Jesus,
> saying, "Are you not the Messiah? Save yourself and
> us." The other, however, rebuking him, said in reply,
> "Have you no fear of God, for you are subject to the
> same condemnation? And indeed, we have been con-
> demned justly, for the sentence we received corresponds
> to our crimes, but this man has done nothing crimi-
> nal." Then he said, "Jesus, remember me when you
> come into your kingdom." He replied to him, "Amen,
> I say to you, today you will be with me in paradise."

As Jesus is crucified, two other human beings are suffering this terrible punishment. One reviles Jesus. The other accepts that his punishment, unlike that of Jesus, is just. He chides the man who reviles Jesus and gently asks Jesus to "remember" him when he enters his kingdom. Jesus then promises the man something absolutely splendid: "Today you will be with me in paradise." Jesus gives the good thief something to remember and to cling to as he endures the ghastly agony of crucifixion. What Jesus promised the good thief he also promises us. We may in our lives have to suffer, perhaps at times to suffer terribly, but we are always to remember: "Paradise awaits!"

The last words that Jesus utters before his death are these (Lk 23:46):

> Jesus cried out in a loud voice, "Father, into your hands
> I commend my spirit"; and when he had said this he
> breathed his last.

At the last moment of his life, Jesus remembered and trusted the Father. He shows us also how to use our power of memory. In life and especially at the moment of death, we are to remember the God in whom we trust.

In treating these Scripture passages thus far we have sought to establish a truth of vital importance with respect to the spiritual life. We have the power to remember and to forget. If we examine human behavior from moment to moment, we can observe a particular fact: we are always remembering something. It may be the task at hand, the hobby we are engaged in, the relaxation we are enjoying, or the people whose company we are sharing. It is on this power, we suggest, that we must concentrate first of all as we search for the divine indwelling and strive to remain in God's presence within.

What we need to learn to remember at all times is that God dwells at the center of our being. As we discussed in the Introduction, God lives in the hearts of those who love him (Jn 14:23):

> Whoever loves me will keep my word, and my Father will love him, and we will come to him and make our dwelling with him.

Jesus calls us to live in him (Jn 15:5):

> I am the vine, you are the branches. Whoever remains in me and I in him will bear much fruit, because without me you can do nothing.

Our first task, therefore, will be to form a practice, hour by hour, of turning our memory to focus on the presence of God within. Several techniques may prove helpful in this regard.

- At the beginning of our day and at the end of it, we can spend five minutes sitting quietly and gazing inwardly saying "My God dwelling in my heart, I love you."

- At the turn of each of our waking hours we can stop what we are doing, quietly turn our gaze towards our hearts and say: "My God, I love and honor you in my heart."
- On the days that we attend the Eucharist, we can sit quietly before the service begins and say to God within: "During this Eucharist let me remember that you live in my heart." Then two or three times during the service we can gaze inwardly toward our hearts and say: "My God, I love you within my heart."
- Each morning we can plan our days of work and relaxation, sharing this planning in conversation with God within.
- Then, during our days of work and relaxation, we can stop from time to time, especially as we take up any new task, and consciously remember God present within our souls.

With these techniques we can consciously train our wills to remember the divine indwelling. Often, in order that we may do so, we may find it necessary to forget ourselves. In the chapters to follow, we will learn more in detail how to be successful in forgetting ourselves. At this stage our major task is to remember that God dwells within our hearts and to strive to make the remembrance of this truth a living one, moment by moment.

We have a wonderful model to follow in adopting this practice. Luke tells us that Mary after the visit of the shepherds "kept all these things, reflecting on them in her heart" (2:19). She did the same after finding the lost Jesus in Jerusalem (2:51). Mary remembers and ponders what happens to Jesus. She keeps her inner eyes fixed upon God. Because she had remembered so often events in the life of Jesus, she was able to speak so clearly about them to Luke. How grateful we are that she did so! How we need to imitate her example!

Chapter Three

EMPTYING OF SELF

*I*n the last chapter we discussed the importance of learning to place ourselves ever in the presence of God dwelling in our hearts. We have the power to remember his presence and can turn our inner gaze toward him. But, as we all know, we fail to maintain this awareness of God within from moment to moment. Something significant gets in the way: self. The Christian life involves a gradual transformation of our souls into the image of Christ. We are to become like him who became a human being for our sakes. The key to this transformation is to be found in the emptying of self, achieved with the help of divine grace.

As we begin our spiritual journey, we become acutely aware of the power of our free will. At this stage we discover that we can consciously resist evil and strive to make choices for good. Often the early parts of this journey are marked by the training of our will to act according to the Ten Commandments and other expositions of admirable and noble behavior. But such an assertion of the will must be only a stage and we soon find ourselves glad that this is so. As St. Paul describes so well in Romans 7 and 8, we discover that by acting solely from will power, we cannot become the good people we would wish to be. St. Paul says (Rm 7:18-23):

> For I know that good does not dwell in me, that is, in my flesh. The willing is ready at hand, but doing the good is not. For I do not do the good I want, but I do the evil I do not want. Now if I do what I do not want, it is no longer I who do it, but sin that dwells in me. So, then, I discover the principle that when I want to do right, evil is at hand. For I take delight in the law of God, in my inner self, but I see in my members another principle at war with the law of my mind, taking me captive to the law of sin that dwells in my members.

He notes that he has the power to express his will (18) but that, instead of doing the good he longs to do, he instead commits sin. He delights in God's law in his "inner self" (22) but, to his dismay, finds within himself a weakness that results in wrongdoing.

In our journey, we cry out, as St. Paul does (Rm 7:24-25):

> Miserable one that I am! Who will deliver me from this mortal body? Thanks be to God through Jesus Christ our Lord. Therefore, I myself, with my mind, serve the law of God but, with my flesh, the law of sin.

It is Jesus and his gift of grace that allows us to be truly free, free from the limitations of the inadequate assertion of our free will. By our own nature we simply cannot become good or holy. Our wills do not have this capacity. God did not create them to have this ability. Instead, we find that in the surrender of our free will to grace, that is, to the Spirit of Christ living within us, this will becomes filled with this Spirit, whose expression is holiness. Thus, St. Paul says (Rm 8:1-15):

Hence, now there is no condemnation for those who are in Christ Jesus. For the law of the spirit of life in Christ Jesus has freed you from the law of sin and death. For what the law, weakened by the flesh, was powerless to do, this God has done: by sending his own Son in the likeness of sinful flesh and for the sake of sin, he condemned sin in the flesh, so that the righteous decree of the law might be fulfilled in us, who live not according to the flesh but according to the spirit. For those who live according to the flesh are concerned with the things of the flesh, but those who live according to the spirit with the things of the spirit. The concern of the flesh is death, but the concern of the spirit is life and peace. For the concern of the flesh is hostility toward God; it does not submit to the law of God, nor can it; and those who are in the flesh cannot please God. But you are not in the flesh; on the contrary, you are in the spirit, if only the Spirit of God dwells in you. Whoever does not have the Spirit of Christ does not belong to him. But if Christ is in you, although the body is dead because of sin, the spirit is alive because of righteousness. If the Spirit of the one who raised Jesus from the dead dwells in you, the one who raised Christ from the dead will give life to your mortal bodies also, through his Spirit that dwells in you. Consequently, brothers, we are not debtors to the flesh, to live according to the flesh. For if you live according to the flesh, you will die, but if by the spirit you put to death the deeds of the body, you will live. For those who are led by the Spirit of God are children of God. For you did not receive a spirit of slavery to fall back into fear, but you received a spirit of adoption, through which we cry, "Abba, Father!"

In these passages from St. Paul we see clearly the call to the Christian: we are constantly to trust in the Holy Spirit. The Church in the Liturgy of the Hours emphasizes this need. Each day, before whatever office we say first, we begin by reciting Psalm 95, repeating the words (7-8):

> Oh, that today you would hear his voice:
> Do not harden your hearts.

Deep within we are to be open to the promptings of the Spirit for each day. But what prevents us from simply living attentive to the Spirit? It is the very self which we need to empty that acts as a hindrance.

In order to empty ourselves of self, there is a basic tendency that we have to overcome. We put trust in this self. It is not surprising that we do so since from our youth we have learned to trust it. It is an essential, although sad, truth that the self develops fully in human beings before they recognize that this self should not be allowed to function as the principal and dominant source of activity. Like the people of Israel, we all follow a long journey to find God, first in the outside world, and then within.

As Christians, we have clearly made full assent with our minds to the truths of Christianity. Once we have made such a commitment, it does not take us long to learn that our wills do not immediately follow what our minds have accepted. As St. Paul describes above, we come to see conflicting impulses within ourselves. Before we can surrender to the Holy Spirit dwelling in our hearts, we need to trust that Spirit fully. And to do this, we must cease to put trust in our own abilities, ways of thinking, imagining, and remembering, ways of feeling, in short, all the self that we have built up over the years.

We may notice, however, that trust in self seems to have led us to certain success in the ethical realm. To some extent we can train our wills and find delight in being able to do good because we choose to do so. But something else occurs when we grow strong in willing to be good. We begin to think of ourselves as strong and capable and little by little we become intolerant of others who may not appear to be similarly strong. We can see in the Pharisees and Sadducees people of this sort. These were good people who longed to serve God well. But, better than any others, they taught why Jesus had to become a human being to show us that holiness consists, not of asserting the will, but of emptying the will in surrender to God's Spirit within. Goodness based on assertion of the will tragically leads to separation among people. Goodness based on surrender to God brings about true equality since we are all equally incapable of true goodness and holiness on our own.

How often Jesus taught this lesson in different ways! Certain of the Beatitudes appear to suggest it prominently (Mt 5:3-12). In these sayings Jesus offers a pattern for living that challenges every individual. In the first Beatitude Jesus says: "Blessed are the poor in spirit, for theirs is the kingdom of heaven." In the word "spirit" we find one of the key words that compose the Scriptural model for the inner person that we discussed in Chapter 1. What does Jesus mean by the expression "poor in spirit"? Perhaps we can approach this question by pondering what persons "rich in spirit" would be like. What comes to mind is the image of those well-endowed with ways of formulating their own wishes and desires, people with energy and strength to put into effect what they think and choose, people with strongly delineated personalities and with many resources available allowing them to define and to determine their courses of action. In such people a well-developed self is present. No lack of any kind seems to be apparent. Such people have the power to express their will in a definitive way.

If we now imagine that "poor in spirit" points to those opposite to such people, what would we see? We would discern those who are not filled with their own wishes and desires, people who do not with energy and strength pursue what they think and choose, people without assertive personalities, without resources to define their courses of action. In those "poor in spirit," self seems small and insignificant. No strongly developed will is apparent.

"Poor in spirit" suggests emptiness of self. Jesus says that something wonderful happens for those who have become empty of self. The very emptiness, the very poverty of "spirit," makes room for something. What? "The kingdom of heaven." What does this mean? In the prayer Jesus teaches his followers the phrase occurs: "Your kingdom come." The picture this phrase suggests is a condition in which God reigns, freely and fully. Those who are "poor in spirit" have made room for God to reign within them. Such people do not assert their will but, instead, yield it in emptiness to the workings of divine grace.

In the first Beatitude Jesus presents, as it were, a description of what is possible for human beings. There are those who are "blessed." There are those for whom the "kingdom of heaven" is present. There is a state that makes that presence a reality: poverty of spirit. As we have seen in our discussion above of Romans 7 and 8, human beings cannot become good and holy by the assertion of the will. It is only by surrender of the will to grace and to the Holy Spirit that our actions can reflect the workings of that Spirit. Jesus calls us to empty out our own spirits, to become "poor in spirit," in order that God can reign in our hearts. The more we empty, the more will we be able to find God within.

In the fourth Beatitude Jesus says: "Blessed are those who hunger and thirst for righteousness, for they shall be satisfied." Here Jesus explicitly praises those whose souls are empty, "hungering and thirsting for righteousness." Longing for goodness in themselves, such souls will be filled. Longing for goodness for others, they will come to see their prayers and wishes fulfilled.

Jesus says in the sixth Beatitude: "Blessed are the pure of heart, for they will see God." All of us wish to "see God," especially to gaze on God with love as he dwells within our own being. As with the term "spirit" in the first Beatitude, we encounter in the word "heart" one of the Scriptural terms that expresses the inner nature of a human being.[1] We recall that we are called to "love God with all our heart" (Dt 6:5). Now Jesus tells us that if our hearts are "pure," we shall see God. What we need for this is a "pure heart." How to achieve this? What is a "pure heart"? We are led once again to the topic of the self in each person and our need to be emptied of this self. With the emptying of self, the heart becomes "pure."

Psalm 24:1-4 describes for us who can "climb the mountain of God":

> Who may go up the mountain of the Lord? Who can stand in his holy place? "The clean of hand and pure of heart, who are not devoted to idols, who have not sworn falsely. They will receive blessings from the Lord, and justice from their saving God. Such are the people that love the Lord, that seek the face of the God of Jacob."

In these lines we find a description of those who find God within. They have emptied their souls and will of all to which they may have been attached, that is, their "idols." They have proved faithful to others in their lives. Once they have emptied themselves thus, they will in turn be filled with "blessings and justice" from God. The main feature of these people is that they "love" God and constantly "seek his face." They forget themselves and seek God.

---

[1] See full discussion above in Chapter 1.

Let us focus more on this emptying of self. Janet Erskine Stuart, the Mother General of the Order of the Sacred Heart in the early twentieth century, had a wonderful saying: "We must be a wild bird's song of praise."[2] If we study wild birds in nature, we learn that each sings a particular song, filling mountains, hills, and dales with different melody.[3] In the case of birds, each sings a song genetically derived, a song that perfectly reflects the divine design. The bird does not know that it fulfills its nature exactly as it pours forth its song. It simply does so. But in doing so, it offers perfect praise to God.

Each human being has a song to sing in the history of creation. When this song is sung perfectly, we become, as St. Paul says, a "praise of the glory of God's grace" (Eph 1:6). Our song becomes the expression of grace working in our soul. We differ from all other creatures with voice in the universe in that we each choose the song that we sing. For the Christian this song must become less a song of self and gradually, more and more, a song of grace.

If we observe the development of a human life, we can see definite stages. In childhood and youth the song that we hear being sung is usually that of self as individuals discover who they are, what they can do, and what they like. Within this time of discovery parental guidance usually prevents absolute self-expression. Social needs will always demand a limitation on the self and its inherent and dominant selfishness. But to a large extent during this phase the self emerges and is encouraged to flourish. As one enters adulthood, there may still be an emphasis on self-expression as careers and life-partners are chosen and throughout life people will persevere in a form of self-definition. Sometimes

---

[2] M. Monahan, *Life and Letters of Janet Erskine Stuart* (London: Longmans, Green and Co., 1922), p. 206.

[3] See the wonderful book by Lang Elliott, *The Songs of Wild Birds* (Boston: Houghton Mifflin, 2006).

this self-definition will lead to much success in the world; at other times it may bring tragedy and failure.

Those who have chosen the Christian path will always experience, as St. Paul describes in Romans 7 and 8 (discussed above), a tension between self-expression and the call of grace. In our commitment to Christ we want the "song" we sing with our lives to be entirely one of grace, that is, we want to express fully in our lives what God wishes us both to be and to do. Slowly we discover that by assertion of our wills, by constant self-expression, we may attain some degree of goodness but it falls far short of the holiness and goodness of which we dream. Gradually we come to see that it is not by filling the heart with the constant assertion and expression of our wills that we can come to radiate goodness but by a completely opposite form of behavior: the emptying of our wills and souls of self. We make room for grace to work and to manifest itself. Wondrously we become free of the very self that we spent years defining and presenting to others. Into our empty hearts pours a beauty and loveliness that comes not from ourselves but becomes our own. In moments of complete surrender of the self, in absolute emptying of the self, a presence fills the soul that is clearly divine.

Who are the "pure in heart" who see God? Those who have surrendered their souls to grace and who have become in their very beings the "praise of the glory of God's grace" (Eph 1:6). The song they sing in their lives is no longer their own and yet is peculiarly their own, as that of each wild bird. They have become "a wild bird's song of praise." In Christ they have become truly free to express the beauty and purpose for which the Father created them. They fully express what St. Paul describes as the human ideal: "None of us lives for oneself, and no one dies for oneself. For if we live, we live for the Lord, and if we die, we die for the Lord; so then, whether we live or die, we are the Lord's" (Rm 14:7-8).

It takes long to learn not to assert the will but to yield it up to God at work within our souls. It also takes long to make ourselves stop and listen and then listen some more before we act from moment to moment. Instead of an accustomed pattern of acting and vaguely wondering if God would approve of what we have done, we have first to grow quiet and to listen for inner guidance. We need to learn to trust the "still, small voice" (1 K 19:12) of God that speaks within us. It is so easy to ignore this voice, to follow the desires and accustomed patterns of our hearts, to act in familiar and accustomed ways, to refuse to be still and to pay heed to inner guidance. But when we begin to do so, we also begin to discern clearly features of the self that we have formed and developed over the years. We grow in self-awareness. Then we start to recognize how much within us that is positive and wonderful comes as a gift from God. We honor the talents and riches with which he has endowed us. To these we can give free expression, being aware of their source and purpose. But in the expression of these and in any activity we learn first to surrender to grace, first to listen, first to be empty.

At this point it is important for us to clarify what it means to "empty the will" or to "empty the self." In neither case are we suggesting that people surrender their capacity to will and to choose. Nor are we describing a state in which a person becomes passive, a mere puppet, simply letting God act within. Both these conditions would go entirely against the wondrous nature of human beings that God has created. In the person who has become a "praise of the glory of God's grace", the will is extremely active, choosing at each moment to surrender to the action of grace within and acting in full cooperation with that grace. The process of emptying is accompanied by a growing discernment of what impulses come from self and what impulses come from grace. We learn to resist the first and surrender to the second. We learn more and more to listen to the inner guidance of the Spirit who will lead us to act with greater and greater love for others.

Other passages from Scripture likewise emphasize the need for us to become empty of self, surrendering to the working of grace within. In her Magnificat Mary says (Lk 1:53): "The hungry he has filled with good things, the rich he has sent away empty." If we apply these words to the soul, we learn that God fills the "hungry" soul, the soul that is empty and yearning, with the grace for which it longs. Those, however, who are "rich", who are filled with self, leave without divine gifts, taking only the self which sadly fills their being.

In Psalm 62:1-9 we find a beautiful description of the soul that is emptied of self and its relationship to God:

> O God, you are my God; for you I long!
> For you my body yearns; for you my soul thirsts,
> like a land parched, lifeless, and without water.
> So I look to you in the sanctuary to see your power
>   and glory.
> For your love is better than life;
> my lips offer you worship!
> I will bless you as long as I live;
> I will lift up my hands, calling on your name
> My soul shall savor the rich banquet of praise,
> with joyous lips my mouth shall honor you!
> When I think of you upon my bed,
> through the night watches I will recall
> that you indeed are my help
> and in the shadow of your wings I shout for joy.
> My soul clings fast to you;
> your right hand upholds me.

This psalm suggests that when we empty our soul and will of self, we experience our essential human nature: we are empty vessels yearning for our God. Our entire being longs for this Divine Being, both our bodies and our souls. We discern clearly what our empty souls are like: a barren land, "parched, lifeless and without water." We turn our attention to the One for whom we long. His "sanctuary" is within us! We sense that God is at the center of our being. It is there that he is present with his "power" and "glory." To receive his love is better than even the gift of life. Even though we can be alive without an awareness of God, this condition resembles a barren desert.

What happens when we find God, especially when we find him within, after our souls and wills have become empty? We become filled. Our first response is for our "lips" to praise God. This praise comes from within our souls, now filled with God's love. It is we who utter praise from sheer joy. We find ourselves transformed by the encounter with God within. Actions of the will now follow: we bless God, we lift up our hands in prayer, we call on God's name. We discover that our soul is filled with "a rich banquet of praise" and our mouth honors God with "joyous lips." We experience what it is to be filled with grace and to be activated by God's love.

Once we have found God within, our lives become different. We see clearly that it is only when our souls and wills are empty, when we are like a "parched, lifeless" desert, that God finds room to fill us with the riches of his grace. This grace is like water to the desert. It makes the soul bloom with radiant plants of joy and praise for the One who can transform it so completely. Now during our nights we will remember that the life and energy that we experience during the day are a gift of God, coming from within our very being and transforming it. We will recognize that it is only in "the shadow" of God's wings that our souls become filled with joy. In themselves these souls are empty and barren. In the close protection of God they are transformed and rejoice.

How are the soul and will to relate to God who dwells at the center of their being? They are to "cling fast" to God. They discover that God "upholds" them. Once we perceive that by emptying the soul and the will of self we arrive at a state in which we can be filled by God, we do not fear the experience of desert longing and emptiness. We know that this very experience is the prelude to abundant grace and love, poured generously and eagerly by a God ever present, ever waiting, ever protective.

Psalm 62 perfectly describes the true relationship of the soul and God. It is not surprising that in the Liturgy of the Hours this psalm is used for all important feasts at Morning Prayer. Every soul needs to become empty of self. When it is, it will be filled with God and fulfill its role of praising and honoring God in the presence of others. Transformed from a barren desert, this soul will bring forth abundant delights for others. Ever will it "cling" to God. Ever will God "uphold" it.

Our model for this emptying of self is Jesus. He describes himself as "meek and humble of heart" (Mt 11:28). His own "emptying" exceeded all that is possible for human beings. In urging the Philippians how to live, St. Paul says of Jesus (Ph 2:3-11):

> Do nothing out of selfishness or out of vainglory; rather, humbly regard others as more important than yourselves, each looking out not for his own interests, but also everyone for those of others. Have among yourselves the same attitude that is also yours in Christ Jesus, who, though he was in the form of God, did not regard equality with God something to be grasped. Rather, he emptied himself, taking the form of a slave, coming in human likeness; and found human in appearance, he humbled himself, becoming obedient to death, even death on a cross. Because of this, God greatly exalted him and bestowed on him

the name that is above every name, that at the name
of Jesus every knee should bend, of those in heaven
and on earth and under the earth, and every tongue
confess that Jesus Christ is Lord, to the glory of God
the Father.

St. Paul here presents a picture of what human behavior is to be, an
excellent picture of those whose soul and will have become empty
of self. We are to do nothing "out of selfishness or vainglory." It
is not our self that is to be the motive of our actions nor are we
to work to establish our own identity or excellence. In humility
we are to look on others with love, working for their interests and
not our own. When we are free of self and its interests, we will all
share an "attitude" similar to that of Christ Jesus.

St. Paul then describes how Christ Jesus "emptied" himself.[4]
First, he gave up his divinity, not grasping what was his by right.
Then through the incarnation he continued to empty himself,
taking among human beings, the very "lowest place" (Lk 14:9-
10). He was crucified as a criminal judged by human beings to be
guilty of crimes of which he was completely innocent. Just as in
the exhortation that St. Paul gives to the Philippians, Jesus hum-
bled himself, accepting the judgments of others and looking out
only for their interests. By accepting crucifixion, Jesus redeemed
all people. At the Last Supper he describes his self-emptying as
the means by which sins will be forgiven: "for this is my blood
of the covenant, which will be shed on behalf of many for the
forgiveness of sins" (Mt 26:28). In light of his actions, God the
Father has exalted him forever: Jesus is truly "Lord, to the glory
of the Father."

Like Jesus, we are constantly to empty our souls and will of

---

[4] Cf. also St. Paul's description of Christ in 2 Cor 8:9: "For you know the
gracious act of our Lord Jesus Christ, that for your sake he became poor
although he was rich, so that by his poverty you might become rich."

all self. When the will learns to surrender utterly to God within, to the impulses of grace that the Spirit inspires, then it finds itself filled, moment by moment, with love that pours out to others.

How well the transformation of the will by emptying is described in the following stanzas of the hymn "Make Me a Captive, Lord" by George Matheson (1842-1906)[5]:

> My heart is weak and poor
> Until it master find;
> It has no spring of action sure,
> It varies with the wind:
> It cannot freely move
> Till Thou has wrought its chain;
> Enslave it with Thy matchless love,
> And deathless it shall reign.
>
> My power is faint and low
> Till I have learned to serve;
> It wants the needed fire to glow,
> It wants the breeze to nerve;
> It cannot drive the world,
> Until itself be driven;
> Its flag can only be unfurled
> When Thou shalt breathe from heaven.
>
> My will is not my own
> Till Thou hast made it Thine;
> If it would reach the monarch's throne
> It must its crown resign;
> It only stands unbent,

---

[5] George Matheson, "Make Me a Captive, Lord," *The Hymnmakers, Scottish Hymns* (Columbia, MO: Kingsgate Publishing, 2000), CD Booklet, number 9. Matheson became blind at the age of eighteen but how well he saw inwardly!

> Amid the clashing strife,
> When on Thy bosom it has leant
> And found in Thee its life.

Admirably has Matheson discerned the nature of the will and the need for it to be filled with "life" as a gift from God. In itself the will has no "sure spring of action." It "varies with the wind"; it lacks the power to love freely. Only when the will is filled with God's "fire" can it express itself with its own unique "flag." In surrendering the will to God, people truly find their will: it becomes their "own."

This will of the Christian fully expresses its nature when "on Thy bosom it has leant and found in Thee its life." This "bosom" is the presence of God within the soul of each person. When we have learned to trust the divine indwelling, to surrender our wills to it, we will find "life," the life of grace filling and transforming our souls. We will find ourselves capable of an amazing activity: love. In this emptying of self we come to express what St. Paul describes as the ideal of the Christian life (Rm 14:7-8):

> None of us lives for oneself, and no one dies for oneself. For if we live, we live for the Lord, and if we die, we die for the Lord; so then, whether we live or die, we are the Lord's.

In Chapters 2 and 3 we have discussed two capacities that all people possess: those of remembering God and of emptying the soul and will of self. What we discern is that our spiritual growth very much depends on the use of these capacities. Let us see why this is so. If we look at human lives, we see the formation and sustaining of self is strongly related to what people choose to remember and with what they choose to fill their souls. The emergence of self is a natural phenomenon that occurs in every human being. By grace we are called to discern the nature of this self and to allow it to be transformed by grace. This process becomes possible as we begin to discern clearly what the self is. We can then choose to remember that at the core of the soul God dwells and consciously to develop a sense of that presence. Once we have made a point of remembering God's presence within, we can then choose to empty our souls and wills of aspects of self. Our aim is to render the soul "poor in spirit," that is, an empty vessel that God can fill and transform. When the soul is empty of self, God can reign there, a loving presence that radiantly sheds love to others.

If we glance again at the story of the temptation of Eve and Adam in Genesis 3:1-6,[6] we see these two capacities of remembering and emptying at play:

> Now the serpent was the most cunning of all the animals that the Lord God had made. The serpent asked the woman, "Did God really tell you not to eat from any of the trees in the garden?" The woman answered the serpent: "We may eat of the fruit of the trees in the garden; it is only about the fruit of the tree in the middle of the garden that God said, 'You shall not eat it or even touch it, lest you die.'" But the serpent said to the woman: "You certainly will not die! No, God knows well that the moment you eat of it your eyes will be opened and you will be like gods who know what is good and what is bad." The woman saw that the tree was good for food, pleasing to the eyes, and desirable for gaining wisdom. So she took some of its fruit and ate it; and she also gave some to her husband, who was with her, and he ate it.

---

[6] See also the discussion in the Introduction.

The Devil asks a question in which there is already a lie: "Are you not to eat of any of the trees in the garden?" Innocently Eve answers that the Devil has it wrong. It is only one tree of which they are not to eat. At this point she certainly remembers this prohibition. But when the Devil suggests that her condition will be much improved by eating of this tree, she forgets the prohibition and loses any desire to be obedient to God.

Eve could have stayed empty in this situation. She could have laid aside her powers of reflection and her desires in simple obedience to God. But, instead of choosing to be empty of her own will, she yielded to the temptation of filling. She fills her soul as she gazes on the fruit. She becomes convinced in her mind that the fruit will be good. She delights her eyes in its appearance. She wants the wisdom that it will bring. Her soul becomes filled with self and her will does likewise. Not surprisingly she reaches for the forbidden fruit.

This story has profound implications for us. At each moment we too have the power to choose to remember God and to choose to respond to grace rather than to pay attention to the demands of self, that is, to our personal ways of thinking, imagining, and feeling and to what will please ourselves.

At the end of Chapter 2 we suggested some techniques to help us remember God's presence within. In a similar vein the following techniques may help us to empty our souls and wills of self and to surrender them to the action of grace.

- First, we can do a healthy self-analysis. On one page we can list all the positive traits of our personality that we discern. On another page we can list what we consider negative traits of our personality.

- Second, we can take our lists to prayer, quietly and serenely placing ourselves in the presence of the God within our souls. Our aim, on the one hand, will be to surrender the positive traits to grace so that they can be enhanced and, on the other hand, to empty ourselves of those that are negative.

- We can now make progress in our spiritual growth in very practical ways. Looking again at our list of positive traits, we can group them into appropriate categories, such as traits within myself, traits in relation to family, traits with regard to others. Then, each day, we can consciously work on one of these traits, stopping from time to time to surrender that trait to God within for its enhancement and strengthening.

- We can do the same for our list of negative traits, grouping these into the same categories. Then, each day, we can work at emptying our souls and wills of these traits.

Always in these practices we will remember that our aim is to be "poor in spirit," totally surrendered in will and desire to God's inner guidance. More and more we will come to be empty of self and filled with grace.

What will begin to occur in our lives is what the Lord promised Ezekiel would happen to the people of Israel (11:19-20):

> I will give them a new heart and put a new spirit within them; I will remove the stony heart from their bodies, and replace it with a natural heart, so that they will live according to my statutes, and observe and carry out my ordinances; thus they shall be my people and I will be their God.

Emptying and remembering go hand in hand. We remember that God dwells at the center of our being and our impulse is to empty ourselves as we surrender to that gracious presence. We remember God and make room for his grace. By these two activities we will come to abide in the divine presence moment by moment.

Chapter Four

ATTENTION OF THE WILL

$\mathcal{W}$e now move to a more profound level in our journey to a relationship with God dwelling in the depths of our souls. At this stage we will focus on the two essential parts of this relationship: the activity of the human being and the activity of God. Let us look first at what God does now for those who have made it a daily practice to remember the divine indwelling and to empty their souls and wills of self. Into those who are "poor in spirit," God pours the riches of his grace.

Jesus describes for us what happens when we are filled with God's presence (Lk 11:33-36)[1]:

> No one who lights a lamp hides it away or places it under a bushel basket, but on a lamp stand so that those who enter might see the light. The lamp of the body is your eye. When your eye is sound, then your whole body is filled with light, but when it is bad, then your body is in darkness. Take care, then, that the light in you not become darkness. If your whole body is full of light, and no part of it is in darkness, then it will be as full of light as a lamp illuminating you with its brightness.

---

[1] Cf. also Mt 5:14-16.

God will fill us with his light with which we can shine for others.

The major gift that God pours into the soul is that of wisdom. With this gift we know both how to conduct our affairs in an admirable way and how to relate to other people in love. Proverbs 8 well describes this gift of God (12-21):

> I, Wisdom, dwell with experience, and judicious knowledge I attain. Pride, arrogance, the evil way, and the perverse mouth I hate. Mine are counsel and advice; mine is strength; I am understanding. By me kings reign, and lawgivers establish justice; by me princes govern, and nobles; all the rulers of earth. Those who love me I also love, and those who seek me find me. With me are riches and honor, enduring wealth and prosperity. My fruit is better than gold, yes, than pure gold, and my revenue than choice silver. On the way of duty I walk, along the paths of justice, granting wealth to those who love me, and filling their treasuries.

These lines tell us the nature of the wisdom with which God fills the empty soul. From this wisdom all honorable actions on earth proceed. If we love wisdom, it will be given us to us as a gift. The fruits of this wisdom are far more valuable than earthly riches. It is an inner wealth that comes from this gift of God.

But what is this wisdom that God gives? Proverbs 8 also tells us this (22-31):

> The Lord begot me, the firstborn of his ways,
> the forerunner of his prodigies of long ago;
> From of old I was poured forth,
> at the first, before the earth.
> When there were no depths I was brought forth,

when there were no fountains or springs of water;
Before the mountains were settled into place,
before the hills, I was brought forth;
While as yet the earth and the fields were not made,
nor the first clods of the world.
When he established the heavens I was there,
when he marked out the vault over the face of the deep;
When he made firm the skies above,
when he fixed fast the foundations of the earth;
When he set for the sea its limit,
so that the waters should not transgress his command;
Then was I beside him as his craftsman,
and I was his delight day by day,
Playing before him all the while,
playing on the surface of his earth;
and I found delight in the children of human beings.

Wisdom infuses the whole universe, perfectly reflecting the divine design. We can look at no portion of the universe without detecting its presence. This wisdom was present at every stage of the formation of the universe, bringing into effect the plans of God. To our delight we learn that God took great joy in creating the universe. Wisdom was ever with God and enjoyed being with human beings as well. We are astonished to find that it is this wisdom that God sends into the soul that has emptied itself for him.

In this passage from Proverbs Wisdom speaks further to us (8:32-36):

So now, O children, listen to me;
instruction and wisdom do not reject!
Happy those who obey me,
and happy those who keep my ways,

Happy those watching daily at my gates,
waiting at my doorposts;
For those who find me find life,
and win favor from the Lord;
But those who miss me harm themselves;
all who hate me love death.

In these lines we now turn to the role that human beings have in acquiring this gift of wisdom. We need to "obey." We have to "watch daily" at wisdom's "gates and doorposts" If we do so, we will find "life," the inner life of our souls. The gift is there for us if we are attentive and obedient.

In Proverbs 24 we hear again of the effect of God's gifts in us (3-4):

By wisdom is a house built,
by understanding is it made firm;
And by knowledge are its rooms filled
with every precious and pleasing possession.

Here our soul is described as a house which is built well by God's gifts. Wisdom "builds" it; understanding "makes it firm." Through knowledge its "rooms" are made full of wonderful treasures. Once again we see what riches can enter the empty soul.

In the New Testament we learn that in Christ we have encountered the Wisdom of God in human form. Thus St. Paul says of him (1 Cor 1:22-24)[2]:

For Jews demand signs and Greeks look for wisdom,
but we proclaim Christ crucified, a stumbling block
to Jews and foolishness to Gentiles, but to those who

---

[2] See also the description of Jesus in 1 Cor 1:30: "Christ Jesus, who became for us wisdom from God, as well as righteousness, sanctification, and redemption." Cf. too St. Paul's reference in Eph 3:8 to the "inscrutable riches of Christ."

are called, Jews and Greeks alike, Christ the power of
God and the wisdom of God.

Elsewhere St. Paul elaborates on the nature of the wisdom
that God has given to those who place their belief in Christ (1 Cor
2:6-16):

Yet we do speak a wisdom to those who are mature,
but not a wisdom of this age, nor of the rulers of this
age who are passing away. Rather, we speak God's wisdom, mysterious, hidden, which God predetermined
before the ages for our glory, and which none of the
rulers of this age knew; for if they had known it, they
would not have crucified the Lord of glory. But as it is
written: "What eye has not seen, and ear has not heard,
and what has not entered the human heart, what God
has prepared for those who love him," this God has
revealed to us through the Spirit. For the Spirit scru-
tinizes everything, even the depths of God. Among
human beings, who knows what pertains to a person
except the spirit of the person that is within? Similarly,
no one knows what pertains to God except the Spirit
of God. We have not received the spirit of the world
but the Spirit that is from God, so that we may understand the things freely given us by God. And we speak
about them not with words taught by human wisdom,
but with words taught by the Spirit, describing spiritual realities in spiritual terms. Now the natural person does not accept what pertains to the Spirit of God,
for to him it is foolishness, and he cannot understand
it, because it is judged spiritually. The spiritual person,
however, can judge everything but is not subject to
judgment by anyone. For "who has known the mind

of the Lord, so as to counsel him?" But we have the mind of Christ.

God's wisdom is "mysterious and hidden." But Jesus, in becoming a human being, made this wisdom known to us. No human being could ever have imagined that God would send his Son among us. It is through the Holy Spirit that we have belief in Jesus and in the wondrous "spiritual realities" that he reveals to us. Christ Jesus is the very Wisdom of God and he has been given to us. What we have received is true Wisdom, the very "mind of Christ." What a gift God has sent to us! There can be no greater gift for a human being.

Let us focus now on what is required of us as human beings in establishing yet more firmly our relationship with God within and being open to his gift of wisdom to our souls. Another quotation from Proverbs will help us here (3:5-6):

> Trust in the Lord with all your heart,
> on your own intelligence rely not.
> In all your ways be mindful of him,
> and he will make straight your paths.

With our heart we are to trust God completely. We will keep this heart empty of self and focused on the divine presence within. It is not on an aspect of self that we will rely, namely our intelligence. Instead, with our minds we will think of God and allow him to direct our paths.

What is needed on our part in order that we can be in constant relationship with God within is a habitual attention of the will to his inner dwelling and an eager response to his grace. What is this "attention of the will"? To help us understand this notion, we may find it useful to consider the ancient Greek perception of the human being. One feature that the early Greeks assumed all human beings possessed was that of a capacity of inner vision or attention. The word that they use to designate this faculty is *nous*, often translated as "mind," or "insight." These ancient Greeks assumed that, when *nous* functioned, a person immediately grasped the truth and reality of any situation. What *nous* perceived was always true. A person would know clearly what to do in a situation. The way that *nous* seems to have functioned was by inner sight: it simply saw clearly what was needed or was appropriate.

The Greeks realized, however, that often they did not see clearly what they should do when a problem arose. Their assumption was that *nous* sometimes failed to function within. When they became perplexed, therefore, in different situations and no clear answer came from within, they saw themselves then in need of reliance on other inner capacities so that they might cope with the challenges facing them. They realized that human beings luckily possessed other capacities that provided the ability to deliberate and ponder. With these capacities they could work through problems and come up with solutions. They could draw on their past and consider their problems in light of the experiences of others. These capacities failed, however, to provide the surety that *nous* inevitably did. *Nous* always gave clear and correct knowledge; these capacities did not. Thus decisions could prove wrong and lead to negative consequences. Such would never occur with *nous*.

The Greeks were aware that the ideal situation for human beings would be for *nous* always to function but, sadly, for whatever reasons, it did not. Instead, it seemed to hide and to be unavailable. Its absence could sometimes be devastating, especially in time of crisis. But, when *nous* did function, the individual immediately could discern what was the best and most appropriate way to behave in any situation.

Here we note another feature of how the ancient Greeks

viewed the human person. They assumed that any insight provided by *nous* would always be attended by the correct choice of behavior. Thus the term *nous* came to be associated with what we would tend to see as two separate actions, namely inner sight and the choice of action. For the Greeks, in the case of *nous*, no separation of perception and action would be present: what was seen to be correct was immediately chosen. *Nous*, therefore, was associated with acts of the will based on inner vision.

Of what value will this ancient Greek idea of *nous* be for our discussion? It provides, I believe, a useful way of speaking of the human will, on which once again I wish to focus. In Chapter 1 I suggested a model of the inner person of which the chief characteristic was the will and its essential nature as free. In Chapter 2 I discussed an important function that people can perform with this will, namely that of remembering the presence of God within. In Chapter 3 I explored the need for this will to become empty of aspects of self and open to the infusion of grace. We are now moving to yet another stage in our spiritual journey to a greater awareness of God within during our times of prayer. What the ancient Greek idea of *nous* offers is a way of viewing the will as a faculty of inner vision. We may not ever understand fully how the will functions in a human being. Here we are striving to present a way of speaking of the will, one that may have value for our journey. Once again, as in earlier chapters, I am simply suggesting a model that may have practical results. The model, then, that the ancient Greeks provide is that of the will as something with the capacity for inner concentration, insight, and attention.

Thus, we take our next step in our journey to encounter God within. Applying what we learned in Chapters 2 and 3, we first of all remember the presence of God within and then we consciously empty our souls and wills of self. Now we are going to focus on a capacity we have: we can consciously and intentionally direct the attention of our wills to the divine indwelling.

Like the ancient Greeks we will assume that we have within us a capacity of inner vision. We can turn from the world without and direct our gaze inwardly. In contrast to the ancient Greeks, we will not stand back, so to speak, and wait for this capacity within to manifest itself. Instead, we will adopt their notion but with a difference. We will assume that we can control our capacity for inner vision. We hasten to add that we do not claim to control what we will see but we can direct our gaze at will.

We are calling, therefore, for a conscious use of the will. We are asking that we direct it in prayer to the divine indwelling. We are not saying that we will experience the divine presence simply because we direct our will toward it. Far from it! The great spiritual writers, especially St. Teresa of Avila and St. John of the Cross, emphasize again and again that the experience of God within is a divine gift infused according to God's wishes. The role of human beings, however, is to do all that is possible to be ready to receive the gift when given. Part of this preparation, we now suggest, is the conscious direction of the will. The wonder of the human condition is that there are measures we can take to be ready for the wondrous gifts of God. Essential to this readiness is the development of a habit, that of constantly directing the attention of the will to God within.

Let us examine the two parts of this phrase: "attention of the will." By "attention" we refer to our capacity to focus inwardly. For a moment let us practice. If we sit quietly, closing our eyes, we can direct our attention or inner eyes in different ways. We can, for example, turn our "gaze" upward or downward. The attention that we suggest for our prayer is to direct this gaze steadily at the heart, letting this be seen as the seat of the divine presence. As we gaze thus, let us especially empty our souls of self and remember God alone.

In the phrase "attention of will" we mean by "will" the firm choice to direct our inner gaze toward God within. In such an activity we see that "attention" and "will" have become closely associated. If we join this activity with those we have suggested in Chapters 2 and 3, we can discern important components in our doing all we can in our prayer to make ourselves ready to encounter the divine indwelling. We use our memory to recall the divine presence. We empty our souls and wills of self. In silence and inner stillness we direct our inner gaze at our hearts, rapt and attentive.

Passages from Scripture encourage us to pray in this way. At Luke 11:9-13,[3] Jesus urges us:

> And I tell you, ask and you will receive; seek and you will find; knock and the door will be opened to you. For everyone who asks, receives; and the one who seeks, finds; and to the one who knocks, the door will be opened. What father among you would hand his son a snake when he asks for a fish? Or hand him a scorpion when he asks for an egg? If you then, who are wicked, know how to give good gifts to your children, how much more will the Father in heaven give the Holy Spirit to those who ask him?

As we sit in utter emptiness, focused on God within, we are in the position to "ask, knock, and seek." What we seek is the Holy Spirit, the very breath of God.

As we pray thus, we are making a choice. Jesus says at Luke 12:29-34[4]:

> As for you, do not seek what you are to eat and what you are to drink, and do not worry anymore. All the nations of the world seek for these things, and your

---

[3] Cf. Mt 7:7-11.

[4] Cf. Mt 6:19-21.

Father knows that you need them. Instead, seek his kingdom, and these other things will be given you besides. Do not be afraid any longer, little flock, for your Father is pleased to give you the kingdom. Sell your belongings and give alms. Provide money bags for yourselves that do not wear out, an inexhaustible treasure in heaven that no thief can reach nor moth destroy. For where your treasure is, there also will your heart be.

In Chapter 3, in our discussion of Matthew 5:3, we suggested that "the kingdom of heaven" signifies the reign of God in our inner being. Those who are "poor in spirit" are blessed because God reigns freely in them. His grace fills their souls. In them the Holy Spirit can blow freely. In this passage from Luke, Jesus tells us to lay aside completely certain forms of desire and thought. We are not to "seek" for food and drink. We are not to "worry" about such things, even though everyone else does. Instead, our search is to be for God's "kingdom." God the Father wants us to have this "kingdom"! The Father wants to reign in our hearts. The treasures of this "kingdom" are eternal and "inexhaustible."

Jesus says in this passage: "For where your treasure is, there also will your heart be." If with our minds we value worldly things, if we make them our "treasure" and seek them out, our hearts will also focus upon them. In this passage we can see perhaps in this mention of "heart" a reference to the will. If, in contrast, our minds focus on spiritual things, our hearts will make those things into their treasure. If we practice attention of will as described above, we will be choosing, as Jesus encourages us to do, the "kingdom."

Attention of the will implies that a choice has been made concerning what is most valuable. At Matthew 13:44-46 Jesus says of the "kingdom of heaven":

The kingdom of heaven is like a treasure buried in a field, which a person finds and hides again, and out of joy goes and sells all that he has and buys that field. Again, the kingdom of heaven is like a merchant searching for fine pearls. When he finds a pearl of great price, he goes and sells all that he has and buys it.

Truly the presence of God within our souls is the greatest treasure that human beings could ever imagine. No pearl could ever be of higher value. But, to acquire such treasures, sacrifice is necessary. For them one must "sell all." We must become empty of self, "poor in spirit," in order to acquire such treasures. Then we can sit in silence, stillness, and awe at the divine presence in the center of our beings, our wills fully attentive to God within.

Luke tells us of someone who practiced this attention of will, namely Mary of Bethany (10:38-42):

As they continued their journey he entered a village where a woman whose name was Martha welcomed him. She had a sister named Mary who sat beside the Lord at his feet listening to him speak. Martha, burdened with much serving, came to him and said, "Lord, do you not care that my sister has left me by myself to do the serving? Tell her to help me." The Lord said to her in reply, "Martha, Martha, you are anxious and worried about many things. There is need of only one thing. Mary has chosen the better part and it will not be taken from her."

In her service to Jesus Martha is "anxious and worried about many things." Mary, in contrast, has chosen one thing: to sit in rapt attention as Jesus speaks to the gathering. Jesus commends her for choosing "the better part." What a model for us Mary provides here! The "many things" of our lives are not of first importance. The "many things" of our inner selves are likewise not of first importance, not what we think, imagine, remember, or feel. All the things that compose our self cannot be our first concern. Instead, with our wills rapt on the inner presence of God, we are to sit in silence and to listen.

St. Paul describes what happens when we pray with attention of will (2 Cor 3:17-18):

> Now the Lord is the Spirit, and where the Spirit of the Lord is, there is freedom. All of us, gazing with unveiled face on the glory of the Lord, are being transformed into the same image from glory to glory, as from the Lord who is the Spirit.

Gazing on the Spirit of God within, we are changed. Being entirely available to the working of God, we are "transformed into the same image from glory to glory." We are slowly changed into the image of Christ as we share in his divine life within us. This becomes possible because we utterly surrender to grace with complete attentiveness.

The following hymn by Horatius Bonar (1808-1889) well describes what can result from habitual attention of the will[5]:

> Fill Thou my life, O Lord my God,
> In every part with praise,
> That my whole being may proclaim
> Thy being and Thy ways.
>
> Not for the lips of praise alone,
> Nor e'en the praising heart,

---

5 Horatius Bonar, "Fill Thou my Life, O Lord my God," *The Hymnmakers, Scottish Hymns* (Columbia, MO: Kingsgate Publishing, 2000), CD Booklet, number 3.

I ask, but for a life made up
Of praise in every part:

Praise in the common things of life,
Its goings out and in;
Praise in each duty and each deed,
However small and mean.

Fill every part of me with praise;
Let all my being speak
Of Thee and of Thy love, O Lord,
Poor though I be and weak.

So shalt Thou, Lord, from me, e'en me,
Receive the glory due;
And so shall I begin on earth
The song for ever new.

So shall no part of day or night
From sacredness be free;
But all my life, in every step,
Be fellowship with Thee.

Just as St. Paul does in Ephesians 1:3-14 (discussed in the Introduction), Bonar speaks of the Christian life as one filled with
"praise for the glory of God's grace." He envisions the presence
of God in the human being in the form of praise and longs to
be entirely filled thereby. This will become possible because his
whole heart is set on God. Through this attentiveness Bonar's
"whole being" can proclaim praise. He will no longer in any way
proclaim himself but rather "Thy being and Thy ways." It is not
just his lips that he wishes to utter praise. He wants his "life" as
a whole to be made up of praise. He longs for his every action to
proclaim praise and that "every part" of him resonate with the
praise and love of God, even though he be "poor and weak." In
this way, he says, every moment will be filled with praise and he

will begin to sing the song that will be his for all eternity.

Are there techniques that we might suggest for us to able to have habitual attention of will during our times of prayer? We wish to keep our inner gaze ever on the divine presence within in gentle and quiet surrender. What can help us?

- First, we must be cautious not to allow any strain or tension to enter this practice. We are not watching ourselves or concentrating on ourselves, checking to see if we are attentive to God within. Such an approach would defeat our whole hope of abiding in the divine presence. The first technique, therefore, for us to adopt as we come to prayer is to be gentle and calm.

- Second, we now join our first two lessons with this third one. We begin our prayer by remembering the divine indwelling. Then we empty our souls and wills of self. We silence our usual ways of thinking, imagining, and feeling and place our souls empty and poor before God within. Now we gently turn the attention of our will to this divine presence.

- During our day we will search for occasions to follow these three steps. We can begin our day with 15 minutes prayer of this kind. We can find another 15 minutes at sometime during our day. At the end of the day we can pray again in this way.

- If distractions crowd into our minds during these times of prayer, we will simply ignore them and let them float across our minds like clouds in the sky. We will make no attempt to pursue any thought but quietly turn our attention once more to God within.

These will be the measures we adopt for prayer at this stage of our journey.

Perhaps, however, a question may be appearing at this time in our minds. Are we called simply to direct the attention of our will toward the divine indwelling? Is not something more required? We are keenly aware that times of prayer will be attended also by action in the world. We are not engaging in prayer for our own enjoyment but to come to know the will of God in our lives. That will of God will surely involve much service to others. Yes, we can answer with strong affirmation, something more is required. That is the next step on our journey. The next chapter will treat this topic.

Chapter Five

ABIDING IN LOVE

*B*efore continuing further in our discussion, let us first summarize where we have now come. In prayer we have learned to sit in quiet and stillness in the presence of God within our souls. With our memories we focus only on God. We have emptied our souls and wills of self. In this state our souls reflect Psalm 131:

> Lord, my heart is not proud;
> nor are my eyes haughty.
> I do not busy myself with great matters,
> with things too sublime for me.
> Rather, I have stilled my soul,
> hushed it like a weaned child.
> Like a weaned child on its mother's lap,
> so is my soul within me.

No longer do our hearts strut with pride, all the causes that we may have had to exult in our self and its accomplishments. We have emptied ourselves of ambition and we look on no one with arrogance or haughtiness. We have ceased to trouble ourselves with "great matters," having learned to entrust all such things into God's hands. It is not that we fail to act but we do not do so with worry and anxiety. We do not seek things out of our reach nor inappropriate for us.

Consciously we have placed our soul into stillness and made it quiet. We are not like children who are not weaned, children demanding sustenance for themselves. Instead, we are now weaned from desires that focus only on self. Happily we sit like weaned children on their mothers' laps. We are still and quiet, content just to be with God, as these children are with their mothers. We have learned, like Mary of Bethany, to sit before God, rapt in the attention of our will.

At this stage of our prayer life we also begin to experience what we hear of in Psalm 27:4-14:

> One thing I ask of the Lord;
> this I seek:
> To dwell in the Lord's house
> all the days of my life,
> To gaze on the Lord's beauty,
> to visit his temple.
> For God will hide me in his shelter
> in time of trouble,
> Will conceal me in the cover of his tent;
> and set me high upon a rock.
> Even now my head is held high
> above my enemies on every side!
> I will offer in his tent
> sacrifices with shouts of joy;
> I will sing and chant praise to the Lord.
> Hear my voice, Lord, when I call;
> have mercy on me and answer me.
> "Come," says my heart, "seek God's face";
> your face, Lord, do I seek!
> Do not hide your face from me;

do not repel your servant in anger.
You are my help; do not cast me off;
do not forsake me, God my savior!
Even if my father and mother forsake me,
the Lord will take me in.
Lord, show me your way;
lead me on a level path
    because of my enemies.
Do not abandon me to the will of my foes;
malicious and lying witnesses
    have risen against me.
But I believe I shall enjoy the Lord's goodness
in the land of the living.
Wait for the Lord, take courage;
be stouthearted, wait for the Lord!

We now find within our hearts the "house" and "shelter" of the Lord. The "one thing" that we long for is to abide there ever. We want to encounter God within, "to gaze at his beauty." In this inner shrine we will find "refuge" for times of trouble. It will be for us a "rock" set above troubled waters. In this shelter we will be joyous, constantly praising and singing to God.

Wonder of wonders, we feel ourselves called to this intimate form of prayer. "Seek his face," our hearts tell us. As we sit in silence and stillness, it may not always happen that we find the face of God but we will nonetheless continue faithful to our prayer. From the experience of our own lives we will learn to "wait for the Lord." Courage will prevent us from wavering in our conviction that we are where we have been called to be: steady in prayer to God within.

As we practice more and more our three steps of remembering God's presence, of emptying our souls and wills of self, and of directing the attention of our wills to God within, it will seem to us that we have found a new shelter at our centers (Ps 91):

> We who dwell in the shelter of the Most High,
> who abide in the shadow of the Almighty,
> Say to the Lord, "My refuge and fortress,
> my God in whom I trust."
> God will rescue us from the fowler's snare,
> from the destroying plague,
> Will shelter us with his pinions,
> spread wings that we may take refuge.
> God's faithfulness is a protecting shield.
>
> We shall not fear the terror of the night
> nor the arrow that flies by day.
> Though a thousand fall at our side,
> ten thousand at our right hand,
> Near us it shall not come.
>
> We need simply watch;
> the punishment of the wicked we will see.
> We have the Lord for our refuge;
> we have made the Most High our stronghold.
> No evil shall befall us,
> no affliction come near our tent.
>
> For God commands the angels
> to guard us in all our ways.
> With their hands they shall support us,
> lest we strike our foot against a stone.
> We shall tread upon the asp and the viper,
> trample the lion and the dragon.
>
> "Whoever clings to me I will deliver;
> whoever knows my name I will set on high.
> All who call upon me I will answer;

I will be with them in distress;
I will deliver them and give them honor.
With length of days I will satisfy them
and show them my saving power."

What joy we feel as we realize that God has called us to be among those "who dwell in the shelter of the Most High, and abide in the shadow of the Almighty." And we have been called thus as we strive to encounter God within. We can truly say to God: "my refuge and fortress, my God in whom I trust." We have emptied ourselves of self and turned to the divine as the source of our strength. Now we discover that we are protected by God's "shield." We find ourselves protected from harm that could befall us from without. God has freed us from fear because he is now our "stronghold."

God's angels keep us safe. We go forth to carry out our duties and find that we are able to perform wondrous feats in danger as we strive to fight evil in the world. We have learned to "cling" to God and he will never fail us. As we persevere in striving to find and to abide in the divine presence within, God will be with us every step of the way.

We are now ready to answer the question posed at the end of the last chapter: Are we called simply to direct the attention of our will to the divine indwelling or is something more required? Yes, something more is needed and is related to the very essence of the will. The chief and most important function of the human will is to express love. Human beings are called to use their wills in the most astounding way: they are to fall in love with God! The most amazing capacity of the human will is that it can love. If we review our lives, we see that this will, active from our first moments, has shown itself capable of making countless types of choices. We have seen that for each person the choices made by the will over the years have established the self. Each of us has learned that certain choices made by the will lead us nearer to God, especially God within. Others lead us away from God, establishing an identity alien to and distant from God.

Thus far we have seen very clearly that the will can make choices. We have seen it able to direct the memory to God within. We have seen it choose to become empty of self. We have suggested that it can direct its attention inward to God. Now we suggest that the most important thing that the will can choose is to love. It is in understanding this feature of the will that we can begin to understand more deeply the nature of this most important of gifts that God gave to human beings. God could have created us to be creatures without free will. We could have been made to be perfectly obedient, fulfilling exactly God's every wish and desire for us. We believe firmly that God wishes only good for us. As creatures without free will, we would have been able to respond to God's will without hindrance. We would have been perfect sons and daughters of God. But, if we had been created thus, we could not have established a relationship of love with him. For a loving relationship to exist, there must be freedom of choice. If one acts out of duty or necessity, that is not love.

As discussed in the Introduction, God created human beings in his own image. The most important feature of that image is that we can choose to love. With our wills we can respond fully to another, first to God and then to neighbor. When God entered human history and revealed his presence, his first request was that we love him. The very essence of Judaism and Christianity is that we are called to love (Dt 6:5, Mk 12:28-31).[1]

As we now sit before the divine presence in our souls, we begin to grasp what love is. It is a complete emptying into the Other, longing only for the delight and joy of the Other. We realize that this emptying of the will for another is how we are also

---

[1] See the discussion of these passages in the Introduction.

to love our neighbor. The action of the will is the same: we pour out everything as gift. As we engage thus in prayer we experience something else: the more we pour out our wills in love for God the more we are filled by his divine presence. We become empty and we are filled! We have discovered, like Mary of Bethany, the "one thing necessary" in our relationship with God (Lk 10:42): LOVE.

What then are human beings called to do? To fall in love with God! We come to understand that God dwells in the center of our being and that his being is Love itself. How well now the words of the First Letter of John take on a rich meaning for us. John tells us who we are (3:1-2):

> See what love the Father has bestowed on us that we may be called the children of God. Yet so we are. The reason the world does not know us is that it did not know him. Beloved, we are God's children now; what we shall be has not yet been revealed. We do know that when it is revealed we shall be like him, for we shall see him as he is.

In our moments of prayer, in stillness and silence before God within, we recognize that we are "children of God." We have been chosen to abide in a special relationship with God. Our destiny will be to be "like him" when we come to "see him as he is." In light of this identity, our spiritual journey thus far has taught us what John also says (1 Jn 2:15) that we are not to "love the world or the things of the world. If anyone loves the world, the love of the Father is not in him." We have emptied our soul and will of self and all in the world which self chooses.

In our prayer, in stillness and silence, we strive to "remain in the Son and in the Father" (1 Jn 2:24), ever falling in love with the Being at the center of our souls. As Christians, we have knowledge of the nature of this God revealed in Jesus Christ (1 Jn 1:1-3):

> What was from the beginning, what we have heard, what we have seen with our eyes, what we looked upon and touched with our hands concerns the Word of life — for the life was made visible; we have seen it and testify to it and proclaim to you the eternal life that was with the Father and was made visible to us — what we have seen and heard we proclaim now to you, so that you too may have fellowship with us; for our fellowship is with the Father and with his Son, Jesus Christ.

John proclaims here what he taught in the opening of his Gospel that "the Word was made flesh and made his dwelling among us; and we saw his glory, the glory of the Father's only Son, full of grace and truth" (Jn 1:14). We know who this Word is who dwells within us (Jn 1:1-5):

> In the beginning was the Word,
> and the Word was with God,
> and the Word was God.
> He was in the beginning with God.
> All things came to be through him,
> and without him nothing came to be.
> What came to be through him was life,
> and this life was the light of the human race;
> the light shines in the darkness,
> and the darkness has not overcome it.

Jesus Christ dwells within our souls as the Word, the "life" of our souls and our "light." In Christ we also encounter the Father (Jn 1:16-18):

From his fullness we have all received, grace in place of grace, because while the law was given through Moses, grace and truth came through Jesus Christ. No one has ever seen God. The only Son, God, who is at the Father's side, has revealed him.

In his First Letter John also tells us how to behave, especially in our times of prayer to God within (1 Jn 3:21-24):

Beloved, if our hearts do not condemn us, we have confidence in God and receive from him whatever we ask, because we keep his commandments and do what pleases him. And his commandment is this: we should believe in the name of his Son, Jesus Christ, and love one another just as he commanded us. Those who keep his commandments remain in him, and he in them, and the way we know that he remains in us is from the Spirit that he gave us.

As we pray, the foundation of our behavior is faith in Jesus Christ. Our determination is to love both God and one another. Using our wills to love, we will keep the "commandments" of Jesus. Thus we will "remain in him" and he in us, seeing his presence in the "Holy Spirit that he gave us."

There is one activity that we must choose above all others: our wills must love. John makes this very clear and gives the reason why (1 Jn 4:7-10):

Beloved, let us love one another, because love is of God; everyone who loves is begotten by God and knows God. Whoever is without love does not know God, for God is love. In this way the love of God was revealed to us: God sent his only Son into the world

so that we might have life through him. In this is love:
not that we have loved God, but that he loved us and
sent his Son as expiation for our sins. Beloved, if God
so loved us, we also must love one another.

In loving we are "begotten by God." In loving we "know God."
The essential nature of God is "love." This God loved us before
ever we loved him. God's generosity in loving us provides a model
for us: we are called to "love one another."

When the fruit of our prayer to this God of love within us
is our love of one another, we will find love coming "to perfection
in us" (1 Jn 4:11-16):

No one has ever seen God. Yet, if we love one another,
God remains in us, and his love is brought to perfection in us. This is how we know that we remain in
him and he in us, that he has given us of his Spirit.
Moreover, we have seen and testify that the Father sent
his Son as savior of the world. Whoever acknowledges
that Jesus is the Son of God, God remains in them and
they in God. We have come to know and to believe
in the love God has for us. God is love, and whoever
remains in love remains in God and God in them.

Gradually our wills learn to love in a perfect way. We will move
beyond falling in love to being in love, moment by moment, stay-
ing constantly in the presence of Love at the core of our beings.
God will abide in us and we, in God.

Jesus tells us clearly what is the nature of this abiding in
God (Jn 15:1-8):

I am the true vine, and my Father is the vine grower.
He takes away every branch in me that does not bear
fruit, and everyone that does he prunes so that it bears

more fruit. You are already pruned because of the word that I spoke to you. Remain in me, as I remain in you. Just as a branch cannot bear fruit on its own unless it remains on the vine, so neither can you unless you remain in me. I am the vine, you are the branches. Whoever remains in me and I in him will bear much fruit, because without me you can do nothing. Anyone who does not remain in me will be thrown out like a branch and wither; people will gather them and throw them into a fire and they will be burned. If you remain in me and my words remain in you, ask for whatever you want and it will be done for you. By this is my Father glorified, that you bear much fruit and become my disciples.

How well we recognize in these verses the spiritual journey we have taken thus far! We have been pruned by the process of emptying our souls and wills of self. We have discerned the working of grace to make us ready to bear more fruit. Jesus tells us clearly: "Remain in me, as I remain in you." Jesus dwells at the center of our being and invites us to dwell there with him.

Jesus in this passage introduces the image of the "vine." We see how very close our connection is to him. We are extensions of him as we share his very life. The fruit we are called on to bring forth is love for others. Without Love at our center, we simply cannot love and all we do is not fruit that will last. If we abide in a loving relationship with God within, our one request will be: "Teach me to love more!" Such a request will always be fulfilled! The Father is glorified if we follow Jesus closely and love much. Then we will truly become the "praise of the glory of his grace" (Eph 1:6) since the effect of grace is ever love and more love.

In this passage Jesus urges us to abide in him so that we can love (Jn 15:9-17):

As the Father loves me, so I also love you. Remain in my love. If you keep my commandments, you will remain in my love, just as I have kept my Father's commandments and remain in his love. I have told you this so that my joy may be in you and your joy may be complete. This is my commandment: love one another as I love you. No one has greater love than this, to lay down one's life for one's friends. You are my friends if you do what I command you. I no longer call you slaves, because a slave does not know what his master is doing. I have called you friends, because I have told you everything I have heard from my Father. It was not you who chose me, but I who chose you and appointed you to go and bear fruit that will remain, so that whatever you ask the Father in my name he may give you. This I command you: love one another.

Between the Father and the Son flows an endless, eternal stream of love. Jesus tells us that he loves us in the same way in which the Father loves him. Here is a love we can trust! In this we are to abide. In the context of our quest to dwell ever in the divine presence within, we see here an invitation to remain in Christ's love moment by moment. This we can do in habitual attention of our wills to love and our complete surrender to it. We will come to live in the love of Jesus just as he lives in the Father's love. Then our "joy" will be complete!

Always we will remember that we do not ever enter into deep prayer for our own enjoyment or advantage. We are there to love God with "heart, soul, mind, and strength" and "to love our neighbor as ourselves" (Dt 6:5). Our love for others must resemble that of Jesus who "laid down his life" for his friends. The fruit that he asks us to bear is our love for each other. He has chosen us for this very task. Being in love with God within will make us people who reach out to others in love and care.

Let us look more closely at the life of God that will become manifest in our being. Jesus describes to the Samaritan woman the effect of the "water" that he will give (Jn 4:13-14):

> Jesus answered and said to her, "Everyone who drinks this water will be thirsty again; but whoever drinks the water I shall give will never thirst; the water I shall give will become in him a spring of water welling up to eternal life."

The water that the world can offer leads only to greater thirst. But what Jesus gives becomes an inner source of moisture "welling up to eternal life." For those who encounter the divine indwelling in deep prayer a "spring of water" appears. This water will be available for others, appearing in the form of love and service.[2]

Jesus vividly describes the nature of the "kingdom of God" (Lk 13:18-23)[3]:

> Then he said, "What is the kingdom of God like? To what can I compare it? It is like a mustard seed that a person took and planted in the garden. When it was fully grown, it became a large bush and 'the birds of the sky dwelt in its branches.'" Again he said, "To what shall I compare the kingdom of God? It is like yeast that a woman took and mixed in with three measures of wheat flour until the whole batch of dough was leavened."

---

2 Cf. Jn 7:38 where Jesus says: "Let anyone who thirsts come to me and drink. Whoever believes in me, as Scripture says: 'Rivers of living water will flow from within them.'"

3 Cf. also the description in Mt 13:31-33.

As we suggested in earlier chapters, the "kingdom of God" signifies that God reigns in our being. Jesus tells us that we will see this kingdom growing in us in wondrous ways. We will grow constantly in our capacity to love. We will be able to be like a magnificent tree that gives shelter to others. We will find that all our being within is transformed.

St. Paul speaks in several passages about what our life will become once we have encountered God within. He makes clear the degree to which Christ is to be present (Gal 2:19-21):

> For through the law I died to the law, that I might live for God. I have been crucified with Christ; yet I live, no longer I, but Christ lives in me; insofar as I now live in the flesh, I live by faith in the Son of God who has loved me and given himself up for me. I do not nullify the grace of God; for if justification comes through the law, then Christ died for nothing.

Grace has made it possible for St. Paul to live a new and different life. It is no longer he who lives in his body but "Christ lives" in him. His self he has "crucified." It is the love that Jesus has for him that becomes everything to him.

St. Paul likewise says (2 Cor 4:6-11)[4]:

> For God who said, "Let light shine out of darkness," has shone in our hearts to bring to light the knowledge of the glory of God on the face of Jesus Christ. But we hold this treasure in earthen vessels, that the surpassing power may be of God and not from us. We are afflicted in every way, but not constrained; perplexed, but not driven to despair; persecuted, but not aban-

---

4   See also the discussion of this passage in the Introduction.

doned; struck down, but not destroyed; always carry-
ing about in the body the dying of Jesus, so that the
life of Jesus may also be manifested in our body. For
we who live are constantly being given up to death for
the sake of Jesus, so that the life of Jesus may be manifested in our mortal flesh.

In these magnificent lines we discern clearly the life that those
who have encountered the divine dwelling enjoy. First, our hearts
are filled with the "light" of Christ Jesus. In his face we behold
the "glory of God." We are still very much human beings, even
though we guard a great "treasure" in our hearts. Now, when
negative experiences come our way, we react in a new way. We
have a reserve of inner strength that makes all bearable. Ever we
die to self so that the "life of Jesus" can become apparent in us.
When it is, we will show forth light and love to others.

Even though we may have come to enter into deep prayer
with God within, we do not cease to be weak human beings.
St. Paul also had this experience and was taught a crucial lesson
(2 Cor 12:7-10):

Therefore, that I might not become too elated, a thorn
in the flesh was given to me, an angel of Satan, to beat
me, to keep me from being too elated. Three times I
begged the Lord about this, that it might leave me,
but he said to me, "My grace is sufficient for you, for
power is made perfect in weakness." I will rather boast
most gladly of my weaknesses, in order that the power
of Christ may dwell with me. Therefore, I am content with weaknesses, insults, hardships, persecutions,
and constraints, for the sake of Christ; for when I am
weak, then I am strong.

St. Paul was not to rely in any way on his own strength. On the contrary, his very weakness made it possible for the power of grace to become manifest in his life. He learned to go totally counter to the types of things of which people in the world boasted. Instead, he learned that all negative experiences, whether internal or external, would make room for the power of Christ to work. Therefore, when he was "weak," he was "strong." We have learned to empty our souls and wills of self and to become "poor in spirit" before God within. The more empty we are, the more he can fill us with his grace, and his power, especially his power to love, can be present and active.

In his emptiness and vulnerability, St. Paul learned another important lesson (Rm 8:35-39):

> What will separate us from the love of Christ? Will anguish, or distress, or persecution, or famine, or nakedness, or peril, or the sword? As it is written: "For your sake we are being slain all the day; we are looked upon as sheep to be slaughtered." No, in all these things we conquer overwhelmingly through him who loved us. For I am convinced that neither death, nor life, nor angels, nor principalities, nor present things, nor future things, nor powers, nor height, nor depth, nor any other creature will be able to separate us from the love of God in Christ Jesus our Lord.

When we face "anguish, distress, persecution, famine, nakedness, peril, or the sword," we might well quail in terror. Our self shudders at the thought of such things and finds itself weak and defenseless. But those who have emptied out self and who dwell with attention of will on God in love, find to their amazement that the love of Jesus within acts as a sure guard and source of strength. Nothing of any kind can "separate us from the love of God in Christ Jesus our Lord." This Love is at the very center of our beings. We need only to surrender utterly to it to be ever safe.

In danger and trouble God within is to be our sure defense. When we go forth to others to serve we are to act in one way only (Col 3:17):

> Whatever you do, in word or in deed, do everything in the name of the Lord Jesus, giving thanks to God the Father through him.

Our thanks will flow endlessly to God because we live and act by the grace he has given to us in Jesus. As branches in the vine of Jesus, we will bear fruit only in his power and strength. In his name we will act.

A hymn of George Matheson beautifully describes the life we will live when we abide in love with God at the core of our beings[5]:

> O Love that will not let me go,
> I rest my weary soul in Thee;
> I give Thee back the life I owe,
> That in Thine ocean depths its flow
> May richer, fuller be.
>
> O Light, that followest all my way,
> I yield my flickering torch to Thee;
> My heart restores its borrowed ray,
> That in Thy sunshine's blaze its day
> May brighter, fairer be.
>
> O Joy, that seekest me through pain,
> I cannot close my heart to Thee;

---

[5] George Matheson, "O Love That Will Not Let Me Go," *The Hymnmakers, Scottish Hymns* (Columbia, MO: Kingsgate Publishing, 2000), CD Booklet, number 11.

I trace the rainbow through the rain,
And feel the promise is not vain
That morn shall tearless be.

O cross, that liftest up my head,
I dare not ask to fly from thee;
I lay in dust life's glory dead,
And from the ground there blossoms red
Life that shall endless be.

First, we rest in Love, surrendering to it our life that it may be enriched by the "ocean depths" of God's love. Then, to divine Light we yield up our hearts empty so that in them the light "borrowed" from God may beam forth more brightly. In our pain we will remember divine Joy and cling with our memory to the promise of a "tearless morn." In our suffering we will cling to the cross, knowing that through it is the entrance to eternal life.

A GAZE OF LOVE

*T*he purpose of this book has been to suggest steps by which we can discover and relate to the divine presence at the core of our beings. We have suggested techniques to start us on our journey and to help us on our way. We described the different words found in Scripture that refer to the inner structure of human beings, many of which occurred again and again in the quotations that we introduced. In the model we adopted, our focus was on one aspect of the human being, namely our gift of free will. It is the action of our wills that is of prime importance at every step of our spiritual journey.

With the will we can learn constantly to remember the presence of God within not only during our times of prayer but at all times. Once we have established this practice, we can learn to discern aspects of our self, those that are positive and those that are negative. We can choose to empty our souls and will of self, presenting ourselves "poor in spirit" before God. In prayer we can come to direct the attention of our will on the divine presence. With this will we can fall in love with God and gradually learn to be endlessly in love with Love at the center of our being. Ideally, our life will become a gaze of love at Love itself.

Having said all these things, we wish now to emphasize a

most important truth: God is mystery and his presence within us is also a great mystery. As mentioned before, we can never guarantee that in our prayer we will encounter God. The gift of the awareness of his presence is his alone. It is a grace that he gives and it is by grace that he acts. Our role as human beings is to make ourselves ready to receive the gift. We become the empty vessels that he can fill. Sometimes it may be that he leaves the vessels empty but at such times we must remain available to his actions. We must not turn to be filled by other things that our self may choose or that the world might recommend. We have to abide in peace and serenity, longing for Love to fill what is his own to use.

Sometimes our prayer experience will be wonderful beyond words. We will hear the voice of our Beloved calling to us (Song of Songs 2:10-14):

> Arise, my beloved, my beautiful one, and come!
> For see, the winter is past, the rains are over and gone.
> The flowers appear on the earth,
> the time of pruning the vines has come, and
> the song of the dove is heard in our land.
> The fig tree puts forth its figs,
> and the vines, in bloom, give forth fragrance.
> Arise, my beloved, my beautiful one, and come!
> O my dove in the clefts of the rock,
> in the secret recesses of the cliff,
> Let me see you, let me hear your voice,
> For your voice is sweet, and you are lovely.

As we sit silently in prayer, we find God within. Our souls becomes filled with divine richness just as the world bursts forth with beauty in the springtime. We sense how beautiful as creatures are the empty soul and attentive will with which we have come to prayer. We feel that God finds us "lovely" and longs to fill us with his presence. With all our will we "arise and come." Love is truly present to us and we eagerly respond to his call.

Then our prayer becomes a rich banquet for our soul, as we heard in Psalm 63:6: "My soul shall savor the rich banquet of praise." With the bride in the Song of Songs we exclaim (2:3): "I delight to rest in his shadow and his fruit is sweet to my taste." We have found the One we love.

But in prayer it is not always thus. At other times we may have done all we can to be ready for the divine encounter but instead of richness we find nothing. Then our experience resembles that of Psalm 63:2: "For you my soul thirsts, like a land parched, lifeless, and without water." We experience to the full our own emptiness and dryness. "Where is God," we cry out? With the bride in the Song of Songs we can say (3:1): "I sought him whom my heart loves; I sought him and did not find him." At such times we begin to understand what faith is. We grasp what it means to be steady and sure. We learn actively to choose to do what Jesus so deeply longed for his disciples to do in Gethsemane, "to watch with him" in prayer (Mt 26:36-45). In his hour of suffering Jesus greatly needed the support of his disciples but sadly, in weakness, they fell asleep, not once only but three times. When in our prayer we feel completely alone, we must then especially pray for the grace to remain faithful and true. Then in particular we will recall the words of Dag Hammarskjold: "I am the vessel. The draft is God's. And God is the thirsty one."[1]

We simply cannot understand why our prayer differs in these ways. But God tells us (Is 55:8): "My thoughts are not your thoughts, nor are your ways my ways." We must trust the mystery of God, fully confident that he loves us and wants only our good. What we are called to do by God is clear (Pr 23:26): "My child,

---

[1] *Markings* (New York: Alfred A. Knopf, 1965), p. 91.

give me your heart and let your eyes be attentive to my ways." We surrender our will in love to God and leave all to him who is Love itself. It may be that in our lives we will experience what God said to Isaiah (48:10): "See I have refined you like silver, tested you in the furnace of affliction."

But we will have confidence in what God also told Isaiah (48:17-18):

> Thus says the Lord, your redeemer, the Holy One of Israel: I, the Lord, your God, teach you what is for your good, and lead you on the way you should go. If you would hearken to my commandments, your prosperity would be like a river, and your vindication like the waves of the sea.

In periods of dryness we trust that God will once again shed the brightness of his presence into our souls.

Let us give an overview of who we are called to be as human beings, seen now as those called to be in an intimate relationship with God dwelling at the core of our being. St. Paul tells us (2 Cor 5:17):

> Whoever is in Christ is a new creation: the old things have passed away; behold, new things have come.

Our experience of Christian prayer makes us into an entirely "new creation." We can let everything go! We empty our souls and wills of self, forgetting all our sins and failures. We dwell resolutely in the present moment, knowing that it is here that God wishes us to be present, gazing ever in love on him. We recall what God said to Isaiah (43:18-21):

> Remember not the events of the past, the things of long ago consider not; See, I am doing something

new! Now it springs forth, do you not perceive it? In the desert I make a way, in the wasteland, rivers. Wild beasts honor me, jackals and ostriches, For I put water in the desert and rivers in the wasteland for my chosen people to drink, The people whom I formed for myself, that they might announce my praise.

How this passage sums up our new existence! We trust that God is constantly "doing something new." In our souls which have become as empty as a desert, he makes a "way." Into our emptiness he makes "rivers" of grace flow. We are being formed into a "people" for God, so that we "might announce" his praise. As St. Paul aptly says (Eph 1:6), we become the "praise of the glory of his grace."

In another passage St. Paul presents a different image of us (2 Cor 2:15):

> But thanks be to God, who always leads us in triumph in Christ and manifests through us the odor of the knowledge of him in every place. For we are the aroma of Christ for God among those who are being saved and among those who are perishing.

As people who constantly recognize the presence of God within we have become "the aroma of Christ for God." We send forth one fragrance only, that of love. Thus we are to do as St. Paul also says and imitate Christ (Eph 5:2): "Live in love, as Christ loved us and handed himself over for us as a sacrificial offering to God for a fragrant aroma."

In Ephesians St. Paul also sums up perfectly what we have become (2:8-10)[2]:

---

[2]   See also the discussion of this passage in the Introduction.

> For by grace you have been saved through faith, and this is not from you; it is the gift of God; it is not from works, so no one may boast. For we are his handiwork, created in Christ Jesus for the good works that God has prepared in advance, that we should live in them.

We know that even though we have diligently adopted all measures that will make us ready for prayer, it is not our work that we can love. It is a gift of grace. We have surrendered our wills to God within so that he can fashion us as he wishes. We become entirely his "handiwork." It is in Christ Jesus that we are created and transformed. It is for a purpose that all this takes place. There are "good works" for us to perform, waiting for us, so that we might "live in them." We are completely and thoroughly loved, each given a purpose in life to love and serve others.

How fully we now comprehend the prayer that St. Paul makes in Ephesians 3:14-19:

> For this reason I kneel before the Father, from whom every family in heaven and on earth is named, that he may grant you in accord with the riches of his glory to be strengthened with power through his Spirit in the inner self, and that Christ may dwell in your hearts through faith; that you, rooted and grounded in love, may have strength to comprehend with all the holy ones what is the breadth and length and height and depth, and to know the love of Christ that surpasses knowledge, so that you may be filled with all the fullness of God.

It is from the "riches of his glory" that the Father blesses us as we sit in silence and stillness before him in prayer. With our souls empty and our wills attentive in love, we present all of our "inner self" to God. It is he who will "strengthen" this "inner self" with the power of his Holy Spirit. The consequence will be that Christ will "dwell in our hearts by faith." With Christ there we will be "grounded in love." We will come to know something wonderful and amazing: "the breadth, length, height, and depth" of God's love, this love that "surpasses knowledge." As a consequence, being utterly empty, we will "be filled with all the fullness of God."

We can now appreciate the description that St. Paul gives of Christians in Ephesians 4:7-16:

> But grace was given to each of us according to the measure of Christ's gift. Therefore, it says: "He ascended on high and took prisoners captive; he gave gifts to human beings." What does "he ascended" mean except that he also descended into the lower regions of the earth? The one who descended is also the one who ascended far above all the heavens, that he might fill all things. And he gave some as apostles, others as prophets, others as evangelists, others as pastors and teachers, to equip the holy ones for the work of ministry, for building up the body of Christ, until we all attain to the unity of faith and knowledge of the Son of God, to mature manhood, to the extent of the full stature of Christ, so that we may no longer be infants, tossed by waves and swept along by every wind of teaching arising from human trickery, from their cunning in the interests of deceitful scheming. Rather, living the truth in love, we should grow in every way into him who is the head, Christ, from whom the whole body, joined and held together by every supporting ligament, with the proper functioning of each part, brings about the body's growth and builds itself up in love.

Our mission is clear. Each of us has been granted grace to fulfill a specific purpose. For whatever we have been called to do, inwardly we are all called to profound prayer in the presence of God within. Through such prayer we can daily aspire to "attain to the unity of faith and knowledge of the Son of God, to mature manhood, to the extent of the full stature of Christ." What we will strive to do, gently and quietly, is to live "the truth in love." Acting thus, we will "grow in every way into him who is the head, Christ." Truly then Jesus will be the "vine" and we, "the branches" (Jn 15:1-5).

A beautiful hymn of George Matheson well expresses our experience of finding God within and gazing on him in love[3]:

> O Love of God, how strong and true;
> Eternal, and yet ever new;
> Uncomprehended and unbought,
> Beyond all knowledge and all thought!
>
> O Love of God, how deep and great,
> Far deeper than man's deepest hate;
> Self-fed, self-kindled like the light,
> Changeless, eternal, infinite.
>
> O wide-embracing, wondrous Love,
> We read thee in the sky above;
> We read thee in the earth below,
> In seas that swell and streams that flow.
>
> O Love of God, our shield and stay
> Through all the perils of our way;
> Eternal Love, in thee we rest,
> For ever safe, for ever blest.

---

[3] George Matheson, "O Love of God, How Strong and True," *The Hymnmakers, Scottish Hymns* (Columbia, MO: Kingsgate Publishing, 2000), CD Booklet, number 10.

SUGGESTED READING

$\mathcal{F}$or those who wish to learn more about the Divine Indwelling, excellent resources are the works of St. Teresa of Avila, Blessed Elizabeth of the Trinity, and St. John of the Cross.

St. Teresa of Avila

Translations:

The Collected Works of St. Teresa of Avila, trans. K. Kavanaugh, OCD and O. Rodriguez, OCD (Washington, DC: ICS Publications, 1987), 2nd ed. 3 Volumes.

The Letters of Saint Teresa of Jesus, trans. K. Kavanaugh, OCD (Washington: ICS Publications, 2001). Volume 1.

The Complete Works of St. Teresa of Avila, trans. E.A. Peers (London: Sheed and Ward, 1946), 3 Volumes.

The Letters of Saint Teresa of Jesus, trans. E.A. Peers (Westminster, MD: Newman Press, 1950).

The Prayers of Teresa of Avila, trans. and edited T. Alvarez, OCD (Hyde Park, NY: New City Press, 1990).

Blessed Elizabeth of the Trinity

Translations:

The Complete Works of Elizabeth of the Trinity, Vol. I, trans. by A. Kane (Washington, DC: ICS Publications, 1984).

The Complete Works of Elizabeth of the Trinity, Vol. II, trans. by A.E. Nash (Washington, DC: ICS Publications, 1995).

St. John of the Cross

Translations:

The Living Flame of Love, Versions A and B, trans. Jane Ackerman (Binghamton, NY: Medieval and Renaissance Texts and Studies, 1995).

Poems of St. John of the Cross, trans. Roy Campbell (New York: Pantheon, 1951).

The Poems of St. John of the Cross, trans. K. Jones, English and Spanish (Tunbridge Wells: Burns and Oates, 1993).

The Complete Works of St. John of the Cross, trans. K. Kavanaugh, OCD and O. Rodriguez, OCD (Washington, DC: ICS Publications, 1991).

The Poems of St. John of the Cross, trans. K. Krabhenhoft (New York: Harcourt, Brace and Co. 1999).

The Complete Works of Saint John of the Cross, trans. E.A. Peers (London: Burns and Oates, 1964), 3 Vols.

The Prayers of John of the Cross, trans. A. Ruiz, OCD (Hyde Park, NY: New City Press, 1991).

J. Steuart, SJ. *The Mystical Doctrine of St. John of the Cross*, trans. D. Lewis (London, 1974).

Index of Scripture Passages Discussed

ST PAULS

This book was produced by ST PAULS/Alba House, the Society of St. Paul, an international religious congregation of priests and brothers dedicated to serving the Church through the communications media.

For information regarding this and associated ministries of the Pauline Family of Congregations, write to the Vocation Director, Society of St. Paul, 2187 Victory Blvd., Staten Island, New York 10314-6603. Phone (718) 982-5709; or E-mail: vocation@stpauls.us or check our internet site, www.vocationoffice.org